MW01293792

THE JUSTICE OF GOD

OTHER BOOKS BY DR. JOE IBOJIE

Bible-Based Dictionary of Prophetic Symbols for Every Christian—New

The Watchman—New

Dreams and Visions Volume 1—
International Best Seller

Dreams and Visions Volume 2—New

How to Live the Supernatural Life in the Here and Now—
International Best Seller

Illustrated Bible-Based Dictionary of Dream Symbols—
International Best Seller

AVAILABLE FROM CROSS HOUSE BOOKS

THE JUSTICE OF GOD: VICTORY IN EVERYDAY LIVING

DR. JOE IBOJIE

Copyright © 2009 – Dr. Joe Ibojie

All rights reserved. This book is protected under the copyright laws. This book may not be copied or reprinted for commercial gain or profit. The use of short quotations or occasional page copying for personal or group study is permitted and encouraged. Permission will be granted upon request. Unless otherwise identified, Scripture quotations are taken from Holy Bible, New International Version®. Copyright © 1973, 1978, 1984 by International Bible Society. Used by permission of Zondervan Publishing House. All rights reserved. Scripture quotations marked TLB are taken from The Living Bible; Tyndale House, 1997, © 1971 by Tyndale House Publishers, Inc. Used by permission. All rights reserved. Scripture quotations marked NKJV are taken from the New King James Version. Copyright © 1982 by Thomas Nelson, Inc. Used by permission All rights reserved. Scripture quotations marked AMP are from the Amplified ® Bible. Copyright © 1954, 1958, 1962, 1964, 1965, 1987 by The Lockman Foundation. Used by permission. Emphasis within Scripture quotations is the author's own.

Please note that this publishing style capitalizes certain pronouns in Scripture that refer to the Father, Son, and Holy Spirit, and may differ from some Bible publishers' styles. Take note that the name satan and related names are not capitalized. I choose not to acknowledge him, even to the point of violating grammatical rules.

CROSS HOUSE BOOKS
Christian Book Publishers
245 Midstocket Road
Aberdeen
AB15 5PH, UK

"The entrance of Your Word brings light."

Cover, Text Design and Typesetting by Jeffrey M. Hall, www.iongdw.com

ISBN: 978-0-9564008-0-2

For Worldwide Distribution, Printed in U.S.A.

1 2 3 4 5 6 7 8 / 13 12 11 10 09

To order products by Dr. Joe Ibojie & other Cross House Books, contact sales@crosshousebooks.co.uk.

Other correspondence: info@crosshousebooks.co.uk.
Visit www.crosshousebooks.co.uk.

DEDICATION

THIS BOOK IS DEDICATED to the members of The Father's House, a family church located in Aberdeen, Scotland. You are a warm and vibrant community of Christians. For the joy we share, the zeal we use to reach out to the wider community, and for our desire to see the Kingdom of Christ expand, this is for you!

This is my prayer for each of you, *"May God Himself, the God of peace, sanctify you through and through. May your whole spirit, soul, and body be kept blameless at the coming of our Lord Jesus Christ"* (1 Thess. 5:23). *Amen!*

You are the best.

Your Pastor,

Joe Ibojie

FOREWORD

THERE ARE SOME PEOPLE raised up to speak to the nations of the world with insight that only God gives. I believe Dr. Joe Ibojie is one of the voices that God has chosen to speak and give revelation concerning our destiny.

The Justice of God: Victory in Everyday Living gives deep insights from the Bible about how to live in this world, yet not be of it. The truths revealed in this book will bless you and change your life as they help you gain understanding of the out-working of your spirit in a natural world. The justice of God extends far beyond the borders of judgment and dread, it includes the mercy, compassion, and the unfailing love of God—the only real justice in a world full of man's inhumanity to man.

Whether you are an everyday Christian or a Bible scholar, The Justice of God brings to a personal level the fact that God is a fair and just Father. It teaches how you can truly engage the heavenly realms, obtain your blessings, regain rightful inheritance, and work and cooperate with angels.

Dr. Ibojie's intimate perspective of the deep things of the spiritual realm brings them to your understanding with clarity and effectiveness that make them both desirable and valuable in your walk with the Holy Spirit.

As you read, the eyes of your knowing will be enlightened, and God will open wide the doors that have been closed in your life.

I highly recommend this book to every preacher, Christian, and anyone who really wants to understand their spiritual encounters with God.

—Bishop John Francis, Senior Pastor
Ruach Ministries, London, UK

ENDORSEMENT

Dr. Joe Ibojie's testimony and writings have inspired thousands of people around the globe. He has once again, out of his intimate relationship with God, produced a seminal work on a subject that concerns every one of us whether you are a believer or Pre-Christian. *The Justice of God: Victory in Everyday Living* will bless you! This book takes complex issues of life and explains them in plain language that everyone can understand. This book will strengthen your walk with God and lead many to salvation. Topics covered in this book are vital to successful daily living. I recommend this book to every Christian who desires to walk in the power of the true believer.

—Pastor Joe Ewen
Founder and Senior Pastor
Riverside Church Network
Banff, Scotland, UK

TABLE OF CONTENTS

PREFACE

I DON'T INTEND TO WRITE on such a vast subject as the justice of God in its totality, for that would be to challenge the prerogative of the Almighty God; my intention is to bring some exposition only to the extent to which the Holy Spirit has unfolded it to me.

My belief is that the justice of God will prevail and not prove a mirage but a living hope. Every injustice will be accounted for before God from whom nothing is hidden.

Though prayers may remain unanswered, failures, sorrows, joy, and successes of yesterday may be hard to put aside, still it is the hope that the justice of God will one day prevail that gives us the zeal to face another new day.

No matter how bad things look, our God controls history, the present, and directs the future. One day He will reclaim the earth to Himself and on your personal level, God can bring justice to every injustice in your life. Unjust leadership may emerge every now and again and political and religious terrorism may dominate the world scene, but we can always count on God. His divine justice will eventually rule the earth; and for you, never give up on your dream. Though we live in perilous times, though the moments are precarious, I still say, *God is in control.* God alone can make the difference in this world! Our joy and hope in life should not be because we have no problems, but because there is a great God who can overcome any problem and that God, not man or the devil, has the ultimate power.

Today the need to bring the justice of God into our lives has become urgent and more imperative as each day passes. In the present world, anything we do to bring to us the original design of God for our lives on earth amounts to bringing the justice of God to our daily living; the ultimate reversal of the grand design of satan against us. This book teaches how to bring His divine justice into our everyday living. How to achieve this by the simple things of our daily living is explained in this book.

You will learn how things, events, and situations in the Spirit realm can influence the tangible physical things of this world and how the mundane things of life in our natural living can impinge on the happenings in the unseen realm of the supernatural.

INTRODUCTION

THE JUSTICE OF GOD IS UNIQUE. The uniqueness of His justice is that it does not only speak of judgment and punishment, it encompasses elements of divine mercy and grace that reflects the benevolence that can only come from God. God is so unique that He must punish sins, but He is equally so loving that He has provided atonement for our sins and a way of escape from the fallen state of humanity. The reality of this divine provision should also be evident in your daily living!

This is a justice that is shrouded in mercy, compassion, and grace and yet pivoted on strict standards of rights or wrongs and a code of conduct that none can escape. It is the totality of all that God has put in place to ensure everything happens and everyone received "divine fairness." The Bible says, *"Many seek an audience with a ruler, **but it is from the Lord that man gets justice"*** (Prov. 29:26).

In this fallen world we experience disharmony, a far cry from the original plan and purpose of God for humankind. The inharmonious circumstances of this world grimace at us as a bomb goes off in the Middle East, crumpled bodies lay motionless, and crying children wonder aimlessly on the street unsure of what the next moment holds. In Africa, pathetic scenes of starving families and mothers watching helplessly as precious children die from lack of food is a common sight. In the United States of America, ghetto violence is unfolding and assuming an epic dimension;

and in Central America, the ages-long drug war is rapidly expanding and causing devastation in the lives of people, bringing social disorder into a new high.

Many wrestle with the deepest of emotions as they ponder the perplexing question: *Where is the God of justice?* Indeed the prophet Malachi once pondered this same question (see Malachi 2:17). I can assure you; God has not finished with this planet, and we must hold steadfastly and wait on Him! In fact, the Bible infers that God places high premium on His ability to restore planet Earth to its original state of perfection! It is only when that time comes that we can say that history has truly ran its course. This is my conclusion: though the wicked may seem to succeed, their success won't last—in the long run, godliness will prevail.

The justice of God is shrouded in mercy, compassion, and grace and yet pivoted on strict standards of rights or wrongs and a code of conduct that none can escape.

Tough times may come, but *"the Lord is still in His holy temple and He rules from heaven. He watches everything that happens here on earth"* (Ps. 11:4 TLB). The Psalmist declares, *"Awake, my God; decree justice"* (Ps. 7:6b). *"Then men will say "surely the righteous still are rewarded; surely there is a God who judges the earth"* (Ps. 58:11). Even in the days when judges ruled the apostate Israel, Jephath, the Gileadite said to his enemies, *"I have not wronged you, but you are doing me wrong by waging war against me. Let the Lord, the Judge, decide the dispute this day between the Israelites and the Ammonites"* (Judg. 11:27). Somehow, deep within every human being, whether Jew or Gentile, slave or free, old or young, black or white, male or female, is the anchor on which hangs our hope that some day justice will be done.

This book is premised on the fact that God is capable of restoring order and harmony to every aspect of our lives from the failures consequent to Adam's disobedience at the Garden of Eden!

The notion that sooner or later every injustice will have a moment in the court of God is often the basis of our strength to face life each and every day. The Philistines learned this truth in a hard way when God granted Israel justice:

> This is what the Sovereign Lord says: "Because the Philistines acted in vengeance and took revenge with malice in their hearts, and with ancient hostility sought to destroy Judah, therefore this is what the Sovereign Lord says: I am about to stretch out My hand against the Philistines, and I will cut off the Kerethites and destroy those remaining along the coast. I will carry out great vengeance on them and punish them in My wrath. Then they will know that I am the Lord, when I take vengeance on them" (Ezekiel 25:15-17).

More often than not, when circumstance goes against us, we are quick to think that God is also against us, but we should remember this—man is limited, only God is transcendent. No matter what happens, God will always remain the God of justice. There is one undeniable fact—those who work according to God's precepts and commandments will not be disappointed!

We should also be comforted that God's justice is always tempered by His mercy. The prophet Jeremiah had a glimpse of this aspect of the justice of God when he prophesied hope beyond judgment to the Israelites: *"I am with you and will save you,"* declares the Lord. *"Though I completely destroy all the nations among which I scatter you, I will not completely destroy you. **I will discipline you but only with justice; I will not let you go entirely unpunished"*** (Jer. 30:11). The prophet Isaiah spoke of the grace, mercy, and compassion that surrounds the justice of God when he said, *"Yet the Lord longs to be gracious to you; He rises to show you compassion. For the Lord is a God of justice. Blessed are all who wait for Him!"* (Isa. 30:18).

God allows us to brag on this, that we know Him as the God of justice. *"...Let not the wise man boast of his wisdom or the strong man boast of his strength or the rich man boast of his riches, but let him who boasts boast about this: that he understands and knows Me, that I am the Lord, **who exercises kindness, justice and righteousness on earth, for in these I delight**, declares the Lord"* (Jer. 9:23-24).

EXPERIENCE THE COURTS OF GOD

One of the ways by which this justice of God is ensured is by summoning people to a court-like audience with Himself whenever the need arises. He does this in visionary or dream encounters. The Bible gives us clear evidence of these court-like audiences that some have termed *heavenly court system*. I have studied the scriptural examples of how this system operates, and I hope as you read this book, you will become better acquainted and also better equipped to relate to them and perhaps appropriate their benefits.

An example of the heavenly court in session is seen in the story of the divine judgment of King Ahab of Israel. When God wanted to bring King Ahab to judgment, the prophet Micaiah had a word of knowledge about a court session that was held in Heaven:

> *Micaiah continued, "Therefore hear the word of the Lord:* **I saw the Lord sitting on his throne with all the host of heaven standing round him on his right and on his left.** *And the Lord said, 'Who will entice Ahab into attacking Ramoth Gilead and going to his death there?' One suggested this, and another that. Finally, a spirit came forward, stood before the Lord and said, 'I will entice him.' 'By what means?' the Lord asked. 'I will go out and be a lying spirit in the mouths of all his prophets,' he said. 'You will succeed in enticing him,' said the Lord, 'Go and do it'"* (1 Kings 22:19-22).

Notice that a lying spirit was present in this court-like session that prophet Micaiah saw.

Actually, direct references to **court** sittings in the **spiritual realm** are found in several instances in the Bible:

> *I kept looking until thrones were placed [for the assessors with the Judge], and the Ancient of Days, [God, the eternal Father] took His seat, whose garment was white as snow and the hair of his head like pure wool. His throne was like the fiery flame; its wheels were burning fire. A stream of fire came forth from before Him; a thousand*

*thousands ministered to Him and ten thousand times ten thousand rose up and stood before Him; the Judge was seated [**the court was in session**] and the books were opened* (Daniel 7:9-10 AMP).

And also in Zechariah 3:7, *"This is what the Lord Almighty says: 'If you will walk in my ways and keep my requirements, then you will **govern my house and have charge of my courts**, and I will give you a place among these standing here."*

In several other instances, even though the word *court* was not used, the pattern, operations, and subsequent pronouncements emanating from some spiritual sessions or encounters bear credence to the existence of court-like scenes in the heavenly places. The term *heavenly court* is not used in the Bible; however, there are other names in the Scriptures that describe this system. The *counsel of the Lord* is mentioned in the Book of Jeremiah: *"For who hath stood in the counsel of the Lord, and hath perceived and heard His word? Who hath marked His word, and heard it?"* (Jer. 23:18 KJV). *"But if they had stood in My counsel and had caused My people to hear My words, then they should have turned them from their evil way and from the evil of their doings"* (Jer. 23:22 KJV).

Angels are agents of God's justice

The council of God as revealed in Psalm 89:7: *"In the council of the holy ones God is greatly feared; He is more awesome than all who surround Him."*

JUSTICE AND ANGELS

Intricately connected with the justice of God is the ministry of angels. Angels are agents of God's justice. This book teaches on the ministry of the angels and how to rightly engage this spiritual "air force." Angels have fascinated people from generation to generation. Angelic ministry is an invisible but formidable force in the service of God and His saints.

However, for many people this great force remains largely underutilized or may be completely ignored. Many people are misinformed and misguided by human doctrines and superstitious beliefs regarding the angelic ministry. In the end times, God is again going to release unprecedented and unparalleled activities of angels in the affairs of men on earth. Angels are superhuman in physical strength and the speed with which they operate, but they are not gods and are not omniscient and should not be worshiped. Perhaps that is why angels refused to give their names in most instances in the Bible so they are better able to freely act in the name of God. We should learn to work and cooperate with these spiritual beings sent by God to help those who are heirs to the salvation.

Part I

From
PARADISE
to
ENGAGING
the
HEAVENLY
REALMS

1

Chapter 1

LAYING THE FOUNDATION

IN THIS FIRST CHAPTER, I will lay the foundation for how to avail yourself of the benefits of the ways the earth and the heavens interact. The justice of God ensures that everyone receives the fairness that can only come from Him. God's justice is shrouded in mercy, compassion, and grace, but always exhibits His supremacy and sovereignty in a world whirling into near anarchy. His justice culminates in the ultimate redemption of the fallen man and the fallen earth. The ultimate redemption will be to a new improved earth, a new Heaven, and the total defeat of satan and his kingdom. On an individual level, the paradise that Adam and Eve once enjoyed will be restored and even more!

The present earth is a far cry from the perfect world that God created! God made the heavens and the earth by His words and holds them together in a divine partnership. Things that happen on the earth are related to the things that happen in the heavens. Jesus Christ said, *"I tell you the truth, the Son can do nothing by Himself; He can do only what He sees his Father doing, because whatever the Father does the Son also does"* (John 5:19) and taught us to pray saying, *"Your kingdom come, your will be done on earth as it is in heaven"* (Matt. 6:10).

When God created the earth, He made everything beautiful and perfect. God created the universe, the heavens and earth, stars, oceans, plants, birds, mammals, fish and man. All things great and mighty, small and weak, ugly and beautiful, waterfalls, kangaroos, dolphins, butterflies, and much more are all God's idea. The entire universe stands as a magnificent creation that displays God's artistic genius. Think of this, every atom, the spiral galaxy, and every living creature came into existence because God thought of them and declared them into being. So behind the beauty and the history of this universe, there is a divine Artist, the Author of life—God Himself. Every time you thought of or perhaps noticed the unpolluted beauty of nature in its natural splendor that is a glimpse of the beauty of the original unspoiled world God designed.

> The order and harmony of the divine partnership of earth and heavens is governed by rules to ensure legitimate access to operating it.

Even in the present fallen world there are still undeniable echoes from the unspoiled world God had designed. These are reminders of the way things could have been. The original creation order and the splendor that Adam and Eve once enjoyed existed because God created the universe and placed all things in divine order and harmony:

> *[But] in the last of these days He has spoken to us in [the person of a] Son, Whom He appointed Heir and lawful Owner of all things, also by and through Whom He created the worlds and the reaches of space and the ages of time [He made, produced, built, operated, and arranged them in order]* (Hebrews 1:2 AMP).

This divine order and harmony was governed by rules that ensure the legitimate access to operating the divine partnership of the earth and the heavens. God is the God of order and that is why apostle Paul emphasized the need to play by the rules in things of the Spirit and in all things pertaining to godliness. He wrote to Timothy: *"if anyone competes as an athlete, he does not receive the victor's crown unless he competes according to the rules"* (2 Tim. 2:5). Metaphorically he refers to the codes of conduct for life.

In all of these Scriptures, the original intention of God was for humankind to be His ultimate kingdom agents on earth. Man is the crown of God's creation and human beings are profoundly different from the rest of creation. Of all creations only humans receive the breath of life from God: *"When I look up into the night skies and see the work of Your fingers—the moon and the stars You have made. I cannot understand how You can bother with mere puny man, to pay any attention to him! And yet You have made him only a little lower than the angels and placed a crown of glory and honor upon his head"* (Ps. 8:3-5 TLB).

God also created the plant kingdom but put it under the rulership of man. He created living creatures of the water and the sky and brought them under rule of Adam and Eve. Even the animal kingdom in its vast array was to be ruled by man. Finally, God gave dominion to man to subdue the earth and so man became God's ultimate kingdom agent. With this came the ability to rule and subdue the rest of God's creation, including any aggression of satanic forces that may infringe upon the earth and man's rulership of it. Adam and Eve were placed in charge of all the creatures and in caring for the earth.

God delegated to man the power and authority to rule over His creation, but hidden behind this privilege was a proviso, the need to play by His rules. Man too soon neglected this stipulation in the Garden. Man's ability to sustain his rule as the delegated ruler of the earth will rest in his continued obedience to *the rules* of God as the King of all. These rules govern whether or not man will continue to access and enjoy the blessings of the heavens. The Paradise that Adam and Eve once enjoyed was a world of love and beauty, a world without fear, suffering, sin, shame, pain, and death. In order to keep the harmony of the partnership between the earth and the heavens, God also set rules to govern man's behavior on earth, and He came down in the cool of the evening to fellowship with man as long as His rules were obeyed. If so, then man correctly related to God and to the heavens. The legitimate way of interacting with heavens from the earth is through the rules of God who holds the heavens and the earth together. Any other way is counterfeit.

So when man disobeyed God, he and all of his kind were banished from Paradise and all its benefits. Man was driven out into a world full of problems that were not part of the package God intended for humankind. Adam's fall affected the whole of creation and cast a shadow across all nature, a shadow of fear and dread that continues to spread even to this day throughout the world. Unfortunately, the original design of God was shifted; man could no longer easily relate to God because sin separates man from God. Creation's submission to man also became troubled.

Man's ability to sustain his rule as the delegated ruler of the earth rests in his continued obedience to *the rules* of God as the King of all.

Sadly, the present state of things in the cursed earth has created counterfeit ways of interacting with the heavens from the earth. These ways are deceptive and alluring methods of satan and his agents. This book teaches the godly rules of approaching and gaining divine access to the heavenly realm and how to release and obtain blessings from the heavens so that you may not dabble into the strange world of satan and his agents.

Living in Two Worlds—The Reality of Our Lives

In this age we live in two worlds. One is the natural living—the world that is full of sins, wickedness, and all sorts of vile things that are against the knowledge of God, of which the prince of the air and the ruler of the generation is the devil and his evil system. The Bible describes the lowest level of spiritual existence:

*They have become filled with every kind of wickedness, evil, greed and depravity. They are full of envy, murder, strife, deceit and malice. They are gossips, slanderers, **God-haters**, insolent, arrogant and boastful; they invent ways of doing evil; they disobey their parents; they are senseless, faithless, heartless, ruthless* (Romans 1:29-31 emphasis added).

As a consequence, these people grope through the fog of self-centeredness, the allurement of carnal appetites, and the slow death of overindulgence and self-amusement. On the other hand, there is the world that is within each believer, a Kingdom from the throne of God Himself with its marvelous light. As the Bible says,

> *But you are a chosen people, a royal priesthood, a holy nation, a people belonging to God, that you may declare the praises of Him who called you out of darkness into His wonderful light* (1 Peter 2:9).

In the Kingdom of God there is the potential to be released into a life of abundance and a life that is free from all that hinders the fullness of Christ. This Kingdom is also a place where we are able to see the unlimited and unrestricted insights of the beauty of His holiness and the wonders of His love, where we are also able to behold His infinite creativity and the all-surpassing wisdom that abounds in His presence. In real terms, we struggle between the two worlds. The apostle Paul summed up this struggle in this statement, *For I have the desire to do what is good, but I cannot carry it out. For what I do is not the good I want to do; no, the evil I do not want to do—this I keep on doing. Now if I do what I do not want to do, it is no longer I who do it, but it is sin living in me that does it* (Romans 7:18-20).

(For more information see my book *How to Live the Supernatural Life in the Here and Now.*)

DECLARATIONS

"Thou shalt also decree a thing, and it shall be established unto thee..." (Job 22:28 KJV).

1. God has given us the dominion of the earth and I will suppress anything that rises contrary to the will of God. I shall cast out demons and bring souls to salvation in the Lord.

   "The highest heavens belong to the Lord, but the earth He has given to man" (Psalm 115:16).

2. God grant me wondrous spiritual experience in Your kingdom and I will be faithful with whatever You may reveal to me.

   "I know a man in Christ who fourteen years ago was caught up to the third heaven. Whether it was in the body or out of the body I do not know—God knows" (2 Corinthians 12:2).

3. May the Lord make straight the road ahead of me and continually lead me in accordance with His ways.

   "Lead me, O Lord, in your righteousness because of my enemies— make straight your way before me" (Psalm 5:8).

Chapter 2

HEAVENLY
REALMS

CHAOS TO ORDER

TO DISCUSS FURTHER the pattern of operation of the divine partnership between the earth and the heavens, whether by legitimate or counterfeit means, clear definitions need to be discussed as to the structure of earth and the heavens as they exist today.

The graphic imagery described in Genesis 1:1-2, portrays chaos, disaster, and devastation:

> *In the beginning God created the heavens and the earth. Now the earth was formless and empty, darkness was over the surface of the deep, and the Spirit of God was hovering over the waters.*

This could not have been the original plan of God because the Word of God clearly states He did not create earth to be empty; *"For this is what the Lord says— He who created the heavens, He is God; He who fashioned and made the earth, He founded it;* **He did not create it to be empty,** *but formed it to be inhabited—He says: "I am the Lord, and there is no other"* (Isaiah 45:18).

Something obviously went wrong to lead to the chaos described in Genesis 1:2. However, God did not leave the earth in chaos and this is how Almighty God created order out of the utter ruin described in Genesis 1:1-2:

- The Holy Spirit brooded over the chaos.
- The Word of God came forth as pronouncements from God.
- Together the Spirit and the Word brought forth order and recreation.

God created the present earth and the heavens out the chaos:

> *Then God said, "Let there be a firmament in the midst of the waters, and let it divide the waters from the waters." Thus God made the firmament, and divided the waters, which were under the firmament from the waters, which were above the firmament; and it was so.* **And God called the firmament Heaven.** *So the evening and the morning were the second day. Then God said, "Let the waters under the heavens be gathered together into one place, and let the dry land appear"; and it was so.* **And God called the dry land Earth,** *and the gathering together of waters He called* **Seas** *and God saw that it was good"* (Genesis 1:6-10 NKJV).

FIRST, SECOND, AND THIRD HEAVENS

God created an expanse and separated the waters into two—waters above the expanse and waters below the expanse. The expanse became known as the *heavens*, the invisible and celestial realm and also the waters below the firmament were gathered to places and formed the seas. With the gathering of the waters below the expanse, the dry land emerged and that became known as the *earth*, the visible, tangible, and terrestrial realm.

The heavens and the earth are real geographical locations. Apostle Paul alluded to the existence of the *third heaven*, when he said, *"I know a man in Christ who fourteen years ago was caught up to the* **third heaven.** *Whether it was in the body or out of the body I do not know—God knows"* (2 Cor. 12:2).

By this we can infer that first and second heavens should also exist. The first heaven refers to the location of the earth, and the second heaven geographically refers to the *celestial expanse between the earth and the third heaven*. Whereas, the first heaven is the tangible and visible heaven, on the other hand, the second and the third heavens are the invisible heavens (not visible to natural eyes).

The spiritual world is every bit as real as the physical surroundings of nations, snow, the sun and moon, and everything that the visible natural world has to offer.

No one doubts the fact that the earth exists because we can see its tangibility in our physical realm. But the Bible says God created the heavens and the earth at the same time. Therefore, it should not be hard to truly believe that the spiritual world is every bit as real as the physical surroundings of nations, snow, the sun and moon, and everything that the visible natural world has to offer. Indeed, the heavens and the earth are real geographical places even though the majority of the realms of heavens are invisible.

The Bible does not give clear demarcation of the boundaries between the first and the second heavens, and as such there are many schools of thought even though there is general agreement that the first and second heavens exist as separate entities.

Kenneth E. Hagin in his book *The Triumphant Church* writes, "*The first of three heavens right above us is what we call the atmospheric heaven, or the heavenlies. Beyond that, out in space is the region where the stars, sun, moon and the planets are—the stellar heaven or space—which can be referred to as the second heaven.*"[1]

Francis Frangipane writing about the first heaven says, "*The first heaven is the celestial heaven: the sun, moon and the stars (Psalms 19:1).*[2]

The following is my explanation of how I understand the structure of the first, second, and third heavens.

FIRST HEAVEN

The first heaven is the physical heaven, consisting of the earth, the atmosphere of the earth and the sky. The earth is part of the terrestrial expanse we refer to as the first heaven.

In Genesis 1:9 God created the earth: *"Then God said, 'Let the waters under the heavens be gathered together into one place, and let the dry land appear,' and it was so. And God called the dry land Earth."* And also in Genesis 1:15 God said, *"and let them be for lights in the firmament of the heavens to give light on the earth and it was so"* (NKJV).

The earth is the expanse in which dew and frost form, the birds fly, and the winds blow, but it extends to the regions of outer space where stellar bodies, the sun, the moon, and the stars are, as mentioned in Deuteronomy 4:19: *"And when you look up to the sky and see the sun, the moon and the stars—all the heavenly array—...."* The Bible says God has named and numbered these things even though modern science cannot fully comprehend them. *"Lift your eyes and look to the heavens: Who created all these? He who brings out the starry host one by one, and calls them each by name. Because of his great power and mighty strength, not one of them is missing"* (Isa. 40:26).

The earth is the domain of man's sphere of authority: *"The highest heavens belong to the Lord, but the earth he has given to man"* (Ps. 115:16). The present earth shall pass away and a new earth shall be established.

SECOND HEAVEN

The second heaven is the celestial expanse between the earth and the third heaven.

Geographically, the second heaven refers to the invisible expanse that covers the earth and lies beneath the third heaven. It does not belong to the devil; it was created by God and belongs to God.

*In the beginning God created **the heavens** and the earth* (Genesis 1:1).

For by Him all things were created: **things in heaven** *and on earth, visible and invisible, whether thrones or powers or rulers or authorities; all things were created by Him and for Him* (Colossians 1:16).

The heaven, even the heavens are the Lord's *but the earth He has given to the children of men* (Psalm 115:16 NKJV).

However, the second heaven is the place from where the demonic forces exert their influences upon the earth: *"For our struggle is not against flesh and blood, but against the rulers, against the authorities, against the powers of this dark world and against the spiritual forces of evil in the heavenly realms"* (Eph. 6:12).

Functionally the second heaven is the zone of spiritual conflict between the good and the evil forces and acts as a sort of holding place for blessings and curses. It is like a trading place in the spirit realm. The conflict between the prince of Persia and the messenger angel sent to the prophet Daniel took place in this realm.

The second heaven is the zone of spiritual conflict between the good and the evil forces and acts as a sort of holding place for blessings and curses.

Then he continued, "Do not be afraid, Daniel. Since the first day that you set your mind to gain understanding and to humble yourself before your God, your words were heard, and I have come in response to them. But the prince of the Persian kingdom resisted me twenty-one days. Then Michael, one of the chief princes, came to help me, because I was detained there with the king of Persia. Now I have come to explain to you what will happen to your people in the future, for the vision concerns a time yet to come" (Daniel 10:12-14).

David looked up and saw the angel of the Lord standing between heaven and earth, with a drawn sword in his hand extended over Jerusalem. Then David and the elders, clothed in sackcloth, fell face down (1 Chronicles 21:16).

Ultimately, it will become glorious when the Lord Jesus returns and all evil is banished. Then the second heaven shall be no more, as the entire heavenly places will be filled with the glory of God, (the second heaven is part of the heavenly places). *"His intent was that now, **through the church, the manifold wisdom of God should be made known to the rulers and authorities in the heavenly realms** [places]"* (Eph. 3:10).

THIRD HEAVEN

The third heaven is the abode of God and is the home of those who died in Christ, the righteous of God. There are many parts of the third mentioned in the Bible, and among the many locations referred to as parts of the third heaven are:

The Throne Room

After this I looked, and there before me was a door standing open in heaven. And the voice I had first heard speaking to me like a trumpet said, "Come up here, and I will show you what must take place after this." At once I was in the Spirit, and there before me was a throne in heaven with someone sitting on it. And the one who sat there had the appearance of jasper and carnelian. A rainbow, resembling an emerald, encircled the throne. Surrounding the throne were twenty-four other thrones, and seated on them were twenty-four elders. They were dressed in white and had crowns of gold on their heads. From the throne came flashes of lightning, rumblings and peals of thunder. Before the throne, seven lamps were blazing. These are the seven spirits of God. Also before the throne there was what looked like a sea of glass, clear as crystal. In the center, around the throne, were four living creatures, and they were covered with eyes, in front and in back" (Revelation 4:1-6).

The prophet Isaiah also described the Throne Room experience:

*In the year that King Uzziah died, **I saw the Lord seated on a throne, high and exalted**, and the train of his robe filled the temple. Above him were seraphs, each with six wings: With two wings they covered their faces, with two they covered their feet, and with two they were flying. And they were calling to one another: "Holy, holy, holy is the Lord Almighty; the whole earth is full of his glory." At the sound of their voices the doorposts and thresholds shook and the temple was filled with smoke* (Isaiah 6:1-4).

It would seem that Ezekiel described the Throne Room in motion in the visions he received.

When the living creatures moved, the wheels beside them moved; and when the living creatures rose from the ground, the wheels also rose. Wherever the spirit would go, they would go, and the wheels would rise along with them, because the spirit of the living creatures was in the wheels. When the creatures moved, they also moved; when the creatures stood still, they also stood still; and when the creatures rose from the ground, the wheels rose along with them, because the spirit of the living creatures was in the wheels. Spread out above the heads of the living creatures was what looked like an expanse, sparkling like ice, and awesome. Under the expanse their wings were stretched out one toward the other, and each had two wings covering its body. When the creatures moved, I heard the sound of their wings, like the roar of rushing waters, like the voice of the Almighty, like the tumult of an army. When they stood still, they lowered their wings. Then there came a voice from above the expanse over their heads as they stood with lowered wings. Above the expanse over their heads was what looked like a throne of sapphire, and high above on the throne was a figure like that of a man. I saw that from what appeared to be

15

his waist up he looked like glowing metal, as if full of fire, and that from there down he looked like fire; and brilliant light surrounded him. Like the appearance of a rainbow in the clouds on a rainy day, so was the radiance around him. This was the appearance of the likeness of the glory of the Lord. When I saw it, I fell face down, and I heard the voice of one speaking (Ezekiel 1:19-28).

The prophet Micaiah had a word of knowledge revelation in the Book of First Kings of what appears to be the Throne Room of Judgment (spiritual supreme court):

*Micaiah continued, "Therefore hear the word of the Lord: I saw the Lord **sitting on His throne** with **all the host of heaven standing round Him** on His right and on His left. And the Lord said, 'Who will entice Ahab into attacking Ramoth Gilead and going to his death there?' "One suggested this, and another that. Finally, a spirit came forward, stood before the Lord and said, 'I will entice him.' 'By what means?' the Lord asked. 'I will go out and be a lying spirit in the mouths of all his prophets,' he said. 'You will succeed in enticing him,' said the Lord.' Go and do it"'* (1 Kings 22:19-22).

The prophet Zechariah also described a spiritual courtroom scenario:

*Thus says the Lord of Host; "If you will walk in My ways and if you will keep My command, then **you shall also judge My house and likewise have charge of My courts**. I will give you places to walk among those who stand here"* (Zechariah 3:7 NKJV).

Another description of the Judgment Throne Room is in Revelation 20:4:

*I saw thrones on which were **seated those who had been given authority to judge**. And I saw the souls of those who had been beheaded because of their testimony for Jesus and because of the word of God. They had not worshiped the beast or his image and had not* *received his mark on their foreheads or their hands. They came to life and reigned with Christ for a thousand years.*

Other places mentioned in the Bible about the third heaven are the holy mountains, the Mount of Congregation, and the cloud of heaven that includes cities, rivers, streets, and mansions. *"You were anointed as a guardian cherub, for so I ordained you. You were on the holy mount of God; you walked among the fiery stones"* (Ezek. 28:14).

The Mount of Congregation is the center of God's Kingdom rule from where He controls the universe: *"You said in your heart, 'I will ascend to heaven; I will raise my throne above the stars of God; I will sit enthroned on the mount of assembly* [congregation]*, on the utmost heights of the sacred mountain'"* (Isa. 14:13).

The Bible says that the present heaven shall pass away and a new heaven will come.

A New Earth and New Heaven

God is committed to reclaiming this fallen world and rescuing sinful people through His son Jesus Christ: *"to be put into effect when the times will have reached their fulfilment—to bring all things in heaven and on earth together under one head, even Christ"* (Eph. 1:10).

In manner reminiscent of Noah's story, God promises a new earth and a new heaven: *"Behold, I will create new heavens and a new earth. The former things will not be remembered, nor will they come to mind"* (Isa. 65:17).

On our part, we have to repent and turn toward God; *"Repent, then, and turn to God, so that your sins may be wiped out, that times of refreshing may come from the Lord, and that He may send the Christ, who has been appointed for you—even Jesus. He must remain in heaven until the time comes for God to restore everything, as He promised long ago through His holy prophets"* (Acts 3:19-21).

Apostle Peter admonished us to take today and each day seriously, for the day of reckoning will come without notice upon humanity: *"But the day of the Lord will come like a thief. The heavens will disappear with a roar; the elements will be destroyed by fire, and the earth and everything in it will be laid bare. Since everything will be destroyed in this way, what kind of people ought you to be? You ought to live holy and godly lives as you look forward to the day of God and speed its coming. That day will bring about the destruction of the heavens by fire, and the elements will melt in the heat. But in keeping with his promise we are looking forward to a new heaven and a new earth, the home of righteousness. So then, dear friends, since you are looking forward to this, make every effort to be found spotless, blameless and at peace with him"* (2 Pet. 3:10-14).

In the Book of Revelation, apostle John said, *"Then I saw a new heaven and a new earth, for the first heaven and the first earth had passed away, and there was no longer any sea. I saw the Holy City, the New Jerusalem, coming down out of heaven from God, prepared as a bride beautifully dressed for her husband"* (Rev. 21:1-2).

By word of knowledge revelation, the prophet Isaiah describes harmony in the future home of Christians: *"The wolf will live with the lamb, the leopard will lie down with the goat, the calf and the lion and the yearling together; and a little child will lead them. The cow will feed with the bear, their young will lie down together, and the lion will eat straw like the ox. The infant will play near the hole of the cobra, and the young child put his hand into the viper's nest. They will neither harm nor destroy on all my holy mountain, for the earth will be full of the knowledge of the Lord as the waters cover the sea"* (Isa. 11:6-9).

To me, this is eternity to come!

ENDNOTES

1. Kenneth E. Hagin, *The Triumphant Church* (Tulsa, OK: Faith Library Publication, 1993), 11.

2. Francis Frangipane, *The House of the Lord* (Chichester: New Wine Press, 1991), 163.

DECLARATIONS

"Thou shalt also decree a thing, and it shall be established unto thee..."
(Job 22:28 KJV).

1. Wisdom is the principal thing, therefore God grant me divine wisdom
    and may I always operate in the Spirit of wisdom.

    *"I keep asking that the God of our Lord Jesus Christ, the glorious
    Father, may give you the Spirit of wisdom..."* (Ephesians 1:17).

2. I have received redemption by the precious blood of Jesus Christ and
    the forgiveness of my sin.

    *"For He has rescued us from the dominion of darkness and brought
    us into the kingdom of the Son He loves, in whom we have redemp-
    tion, the forgiveness of sins. He is the image of the invisible God, the
    firstborn over all creation"* (Colossians 1:13-15).

    *"having cancelled the written code, with its regulations, that was
    against us and that stood opposed to us; He took it away, nailing it to
    the cross. And having disarmed the powers and authorities, He made
    a public spectacle of them, triumphing over them by the cross"* (Colos-
    sians 2:14-15).

Chapter 3

CONNECTING HEAVENS AND EARTH

WE LIVE ON EARTH, and God's throne is in the highest heaven, the third heaven! To interact, we have to break through the covering interface between the earth and God's throne. This expanse is the zone of spiritual warfare called the second heaven.

The second heaven is part of what is referred to as heavenly places. As mentioned previously, this heavenly place could be regarded as a spiritual trading place for blessings and evil:

> For our struggle is not against flesh and blood, but against the rulers, against the authorities, against the powers of this dark world and against the spiritual forces of evil in the heavenly realms [places] (Ephesians 6:12).

We need to understand the dynamics of the connection between the earth and the heavens so we can avail ourselves of their operations. In the Book of Proverbs, Solomon said, "An undeserved curse has no effect. Its intended victim will be no more harmed by it than by a sparrow or swallow **flitting through the sky**" (Prov. 26:2 TLB).

In other words, a curse can exist in the heavenly places without affecting the intended victim, meaning without physical manifestation in the natural realm.

And for blessings, the Bible says He *"has blessed us with every spiritual blessing in the heavenly realms because we are united with Christ"* (Eph. 1:3). By inference, this passage also shows that blessings can equally exist in the heavenly places and unless the appropriate actions are taken they will not be manifested in the natural realm. These are the reasons why we need to appropriately connect with the heavens in a godly and acceptable way.

CONNECTING EARTH AND HEAVEN

Though invisible, the heavenly places are as real as the visible and tangible earth in which we live. There is constant interaction between the earth and the heavens. These interactions can either be enhanced or clouded by spiritual forces. Also, things we do in the natural world can either hinder the connection or enhance its communications. In the Book of Deuteronomy, we are told that disobedience to God's commandments can block this communication *"And your heavens which are over your head shall be bronze and the earth which is under you shall be iron"* (Deut. 28:23 NKJV).

We can take deliberate actions to enhance the easy flow of divine revelations over a place.

By sovereignty, God can decide to enhance the connection or to blanket this communication between the earth and the heavens, as the patriarch Jacob experienced on his way to Haran. In Genesis 28 we see heaven opened upon Jacob in a dream.

> *Jacob left Beersheba and set out for Haran. When he reached a certain place, he stopped for the night because the sun had set. Taking one of the stones there, he put it under his head and lay down to sleep. He*

had a dream in which he saw a stairway resting on the earth, with its top reaching to heaven, and the angels of God were ascending and descending on it. There above it stood the Lord, and he said: "I am the Lord, the God of your father Abraham and the God of Isaac. I will give you and your descendants the land on which you are lying. Your descendants will be like the dust of the earth, and you will spread out to the west and to the east, to the north and to the south. All peoples on earth will be blessed through you and your offspring. I am with you and will watch over you wherever you go, and I will bring you back to this land. I will not leave you until I have done what I have promised you." When Jacob awoke from his sleep, he thought, "Surely the Lord is in this place, and I was not aware of it." He was afraid and said, "How awesome is this place! This is none other than the house of God; **this is the gate of heaven"** (Genesis 28:10-17).

We can take deliberate actions to enhance the easy flow of divine revelations over a place. By availing ourselves to the open heaven, we can experience the clarity of revelations in a place reflecting the openness of the third heaven over the place. Open heaven can also mean other material and immaterial blessings from the third heaven. An opening of the heavens is the bypassing of the hindrances of the second heaven to connect God's abode with the earth.

HEAVENLY PLACES

The term *heavenly places* is a descriptive term that refers to the invisible realm of the heavens and technically would include the second and the third heaven and other invisible realms of hell.

The following Bible passages give credence to the fact that the second heaven is included in the term *heavenly places:*

For our struggle is not against flesh and blood, but against the rulers, against the authorities, against the powers of this dark world and against the spiritual forces of evil in the heavenly realms [places] (Ephesians 6:12).

His intent was that now, through the church, the manifold wisdom of God should be made known to the rulers and authorities in the heavenly realms [places] *(Ephesians 3:10).*

In a similar manner, the following passages support the fact that the third heaven is also included in the term *heavenly places:*

And God raised us up with Christ and seated us with Him in the heavenly realms [places] *in Christ Jesus (Ephesians 2:6).*

which He exerted in Christ when He raised Him from the dead and seated Him at His right hand in the heavenly realms [places] *(Ephesians 1:20).*

THE "NON-THIRD HEAVEN" HEAVENLY PLACES

I have previously mentioned that the term *heavenly places* includes the third heaven, and so it is important to be clear when the Bible speaks of the other part of heavenly places besides the third heaven; hence I chose to refer to these places as "non-third heaven" heavenly places.

From these passages, it is perhaps clear that the second heaven part of the heavenly places serves as a sort of "stock exchange" in the spirit realm as well as the zone of conflict between the evil and godly spirits. These heavenly places stock both the evil and the good and are trading places for blessings and curses.

Among the numerous happenings in the heavenly places, blessings can be withheld, as was the case of the delay experienced by the divine messenger bringing answers to Daniel's petition:

Then he continued, "Do not be afraid, Daniel. Since the first day that you set your mind to gain understanding and to humble yourself before your God, your words were heard, and I have come in response to them. But the prince of the Persian kingdom resisted me twenty-one days. Then Michael, one of the chief princes, came to help me, because I was detained there with the king of Persia. Now I have come to explain to you what will happen to your people in the future, for the vision concerns a time yet to come" (Daniel 10:12-14).

Curses are also stocked in this non-third heaven heavenly places, as implied in Proverbs 26:2, *"Like a fluttering sparrow or a darting swallow, an undeserved curse does not come to rest."*

Metaphorically, even the dews of heaven can be withheld in the heavenly places, as can be deduced in the prayers offered in the Book of Zechariah, *"The seed will grow well, the vine will yield its fruit, the ground will produce its crops, **and the heavens will drop their dew**. I will give all these things as an inheritance to the remnant of this people"* (Zech. 8:12).

THINGS THAT MAY EXIST IN OR TRANSIT THROUGH THE HEAVENLY PLACES INCLUDE:

1. The dews of heavens.

    *"The seed will grow well, the vine will yield its fruit, the ground will produce its crops, **and the heavens will drop their dew**. I will give all these things as an inheritance to the remnant of this people"* (Zechariah 8:12).

2. Spiritual blessings.

    "Praise be to the God and Father of our Lord Jesus Christ, who has blessed us in the heavenly realms with every spiritual blessing in Christ" (Ephesians 1:3).

3. Principalities, powers, and wickedness.

    "For our struggle is not against flesh and blood, but against the rulers, against the authorities, against the powers of this dark world and against the spiritual forces of evil in the heavenly realms" (Ephesians 6:12).

4. Divine revelations in transit.

    "While I was speaking and praying, confessing my sin and the sin of my people Israel and making my request to the Lord my God for His holy hill—while I was still in prayer, Gabriel, the man I had seen in the earlier vision, came to me in swift flight about the time of the evening sacrifice. He instructed me and said to me, "Daniel, I have now come to give you insight and understanding. As soon as you began to pray, an answer was given, which I have come to tell you, for you are highly esteemed. Therefore, consider the message and understand the vision" (Daniel 9:20-23).

5. Prophets on divinely inspired spiritual encounters.

    "In the sixth year, in the sixth month on the fifth day, while I was sitting in my house and the elders of Judah were sitting before me, the hand of the Sovereign Lord came upon me there. I looked, and I saw a figure like that of a man. From what appeared to be his waist down he was like fire, and from there up his appearance was as bright as glowing metal. He stretched out what looked like a hand and took me by the hair of my head. The Spirit lifted me up between earth and heaven and in visions of God he took me to Jerusalem, to the entrance to the north gate of the inner court, where the idol that provokes to jealousy stood" (Ezekiel 8:1-3).

6. Other people.

    "Paul and his companions traveled throughout the region of Phrygia and Galatia, having been kept by the Holy Spirit from preaching the word in the province of Asia. When they came to the border of Mysia, they tried to enter Bithynia, but the Spirit of Jesus would not allow them to. So they passed by Mysia and went down to Troas. During the night Paul had a vision of a man of Macedonia standing and begging him, "Come over to Macedonia and help us." After Paul had seen the

vision, we got ready at once to leave for Macedonia, concluding that God had called us to preach the gospel to them" (Acts 16:6-10).

7. Warring angels.

"Balaam got up in the morning, saddled his donkey and went with the princes of Moab. But God was very angry when he went, and the angel of the Lord stood in the road to oppose him. Balaam was riding on his donkey, and his two servants were with him" (Numbers 22:21-22).

8. The angel with drawn sword.

"Now when Joshua was near Jericho, he looked up and saw a man standing in front of him with a drawn sword in his hand. Joshua went up to him and asked, 'Are you for us or for our enemies?' 'Neither,' he replied, 'but as commander of the army of the Lord I have now come.' Then Joshua fell face down to the ground in reverence, and asked him, 'What message does my Lord have for his servant?'" (Joshua 5:13-14).

"David looked up and saw the angel of the Lord standing between heaven and earth, with a drawn sword in his hand extended over Jerusalem. Then David and the elders, clothed in sackcloth, fell face-down" (1 Chronicles 21:16).

9. Waters.

"So God made the expanse and separated the water under the expanse from the water above it. And it was so" (Genesis 1:7).

10. Curses.

"Like a fluttering sparrow or a darting swallow, an undeserved curse does not come to rest" (Proverbs 26:2).

The third heaven can be open over a place on a permanent basis when it is called a *heavenly portal* or can be open over a place on a temporary basis.

NON-PERMANENT OPENING OF THE THIRD HEAVEN

The temporary opening of the third heaven occurs most commonly over a location on the earth or even over a person's head as in the case of the prophet Samuel. It can be facilitated by what we do: *"The boy Samuel ministered before the Lord under Eli. In those days the word of the Lord was rare; there were not many visions"* (1 Sam. 3:1), yet the boy Samuel had an open heaven communication with God, though the heavens over the state of Israel were closed at the time.

When the word of God was rare and visions were few, the heaven opened upon young Samuel because he was committed to the presence of God despite the moral decadence of Eli's sons.

In another instance, Peter's prayers and fasting undoubtedly contributed to the sudden opening of the heaven upon him. *"About noon the following day as they were on their journey and approaching the city, Peter went up on the roof to pray. He became hungry and wanted something to eat, and while the meal was being prepared, he fell into a trance. He saw heaven opened and something like a large sheet being let down to earth by its four corners"* (Acts 10:9-11).

There are other things we do on earth that can make God create a temporary bypass through the covering of the second heaven over the earth. In the Book of Isaiah, the prophet Isaiah cried out that the Lord would tie open the heavens and come down; *"Oh, that You would rend the heavens and come down, that the mountains would tremble before You!"* (Isa. 64:1).

Also earlier, the prophet Isaiah experienced an open heaven, which he associated with the year that King Uzziah died. Perhaps it was because of the remarkable success of the infrastructures and the political, agricultural, and military machinery in place during the reign of King Uzziah that the people became spiritually blinded and then became more reliant on the worldly system instead of the arm of God who gave the wisdom for the worldly successes.

> *God helped him against the Philistines and against the Arabs who lived in Gur Baal and against the Meunites. The Ammonites brought tribute to Uzziah, and his fame spread as far as the border of Egypt, because he had become very powerful. Uzziah built towers*

in Jerusalem at the Corner Gate, at the Valley Gate and at the angle of the wall, and he fortified them. He also built towers in the desert and dug many cisterns, because he had much livestock in the foothills and in the plain. He had people working his fields and vineyards in the hills and in the fertile lands, for he loved the soil. Uzziah had a well-trained army, ready to go out by divisions according to their numbers as mustered by Jeiel the secretary and Maaseiah the officer under the direction of Hananiah, one of the royal officials. The total number of family leaders over the fighting men was 2,600. Under their command was an army of 307,500 men trained for war, a powerful force to support the king against his enemies. Uzziah provided shields, spears, helmets, coats of armour, bows and slingstones for the entire army. In Jerusalem he made machines designed by skilful men for use on the towers and on the corner defences to shoot arrows and hurl large stones. His fame spread far and wide, for he was greatly helped until he became powerful. But after Uzziah became powerful, his pride led to his downfall. He was unfaithful to the Lord his God, and entered the temple of the Lord to burn incense on the altar of incense (2 Chronicles 26:7-16).

It is possible that when King Uzziah died, there was a significant paradigm shift in the minds of the people, at least in the mind of prophet Isaiah, to begin to rely on the arms of God; as a result there was an enhanced openness of the heavens over him: *"In the year that King Uzziah died, I saw the Lord seated on a throne, high and exalted, and the train of His robe filled the temple. Above Him were seraphs, each with six wings: With two wings they covered their faces, with two they covered their feet, and with two they were flying"* (Isaiah 6:1-2).

THE ULTIMATE OUTCOME OF HEAVENLY PLACES

Ultimately it will be glorious when the Lord Jesus returns and all evil is banished; then heavenly places will be filled with the glory of God, *"His intent was that now,* **through the church, the manifold wisdom of God should be made known to the rulers and authorities in the heavenly realms [places]"** (Eph. 3:10).

DECLARATIONS

"What you decide on will be done, and light will shine on your ways" (Job 22:28 KJV).

1. God has granted me victory over every form of satanic challenge.

   "For our struggle is not against flesh and blood, but against the rulers, against the authorities, against the powers of this dark world and against the spiritual forces of evil in the heavenly realms [places]" (Ephesians 6:12).

2. I am seated with Jesus Christ and I have all spiritual blessings in heavenly places.

   "And God raised us up with Christ and seated us with him in the heavenly realms [places] in Christ Jesus" (Ephesians 2:6).

   "Praise be to the God and Father of our Lord Jesus Christ, who has blessed us in the heavenly realms with every spiritual blessing in Christ" (Ephesians 1:3).

3. Thank you God for giving me blessings and allowing grace to abound to me according to Your riches in glory by Christ in Jesus.

   "And God is able to make all grace abound to you, so that in all things at all times, having all that you need, you will abound in every good work" (2 Corinthians 9:8).

Chapter 4

APPROACHING AND ACCESSING HEAVENLY REALMS

AFTER SATAN WAS CAST OUT of the third heaven, he formed a kingdom that hovers over and covers the earth. This is the kingdom we have to bypass in order to gain access into what God has released to us. The Bible says, *"For our struggle is not against flesh and blood, but against the rulers, against the authorities, against the powers of this dark world and against **the spiritual forces of evil in the heavenly realms"*** (Eph. 6:12). God holds the heavens and the earth by the word of His power.

There is divine partnership between the earth and the heavens, and God Himself regulates this partnership. The only way to truly participate in this partnership *legally* is to get permission from God. Illegal participation is possible but it is of the devil and is demonic. The Bible says, "be holy, even as I am holy," this is why we need to continuously sanctify and consecrate ourselves to gain legal access into the heavenly realm.

We need to continuously sanctify and consecrate ourselves to gain legal access into the heavenly realm.

THE PROCESS OF CONTINUOUS SPIRITUAL SANITATION

What is spiritual sanitation?

Spiritual sanitation is the removal of all things that are against the expression of the pure spirituality of God in our lives. Man is a spiritual being having a natural experience, so our true nature should be to break the hold of our sinfulness and allow the expression of divine attributes of God in our lives. Before the Fall in the Garden of Eden, man lived in a love of spirituality and a state of continuous God consciousness that I describe as "the realm of God." Adam and Eve had nearly uninterrupted constant fellowship with God and imbibed the divine nature of God that exuded from everything they did. At that time they had no fear, were full of faith, and had the thought pattern of God. They were therefore able to ascend into the holy hills of God and participated in deliberations at the council of Him who holds all things in the palm of His hand.

Jesus Christ, during His earthly ministry, took it upon Himself to drive out all strange elements, put off all strange fires, and cast out evil spirits. These are the things that bring about satanic contamination, inhibit our participation in the council of God, and eventually may lead to destructive processes in our body, soul, and spirit. By the help of the Holy Spirit, God is still in the business of reconciling us to Himself, if we cry out unto Him. But our iniquities stop us from receiving the benefits of easy accessibility to the counsel of God, for iniquity separates us from God. *"Surely the arm of the Lord is not too short to save, nor his ear too dull to hear. But your iniquities have separated you from your God; your sins have hidden his face from you, so that he will not hear"* (Isa. 59:1-2).

We should therefore take solace in the words of apostle Paul as he admonished us to remember that, *"In a large house there are articles not only of gold and silver, but also of wood and clay; some are for noble purposes and some for ignoble. If a man cleanses himself from the latter, he will be an instrument for noble purposes, made holy, useful to the Master and prepared to do any good work"* (2 Tim. 2:20-21). God can abolish every human act that is contrary to His intention for your life. God has rules and a strict code of standards of wrongs and rights that no one can escape, and if we work them rightly, they will work for us. We should be encouraged because it does not matter how we have started, it is how we finish that counts. No matter what may come your way, our God works for good for those who love Him and are called according His name.

In the Old Testament, God asks Moses to sanctify the people in preparation for His visitation: *"Go down now and see that the people are ready for My visit. Sanctify them today and tomorrow, I will come down upon Mount Sinai as all the people watch"* (Exod. 19:10-11 TLB). Those verses establish that sanctification is a prerequisite for ascending into the holy hill of God. Joshua also told the people, *"Consecrate yourselves, for tomorrow the Lord will do amazing things among you"* (Josh. 3:5).

We should pray that God will sanctify us body, soul, and spirit so we can ascend His holy hills, *"May God himself, the God of peace, sanctify you through and through. May your whole spirit, soul and body be kept blameless at the coming of our Lord Jesus Christ. The one who calls you is faithful and he will do it"* (1 Thess. 5:23-24). This too confirms the pivotal role of consecration required of us, if we are to ascend the holy hills of God.

There is also the need to pray without ceasing for spiritual sanitation so that we will be purged from the things that separate us from God and the blessings of purging stated in Second Timothy 2:20-21 to manifest in our lives.

A very direct way of approaching the heavenly realm is by spoken words. Words can ascend as spiritual arrows into the heavenly places. By the words of our mouth we can approach or appeal to God to bring justice to any injustice in our lives or plead with God for mercy, which is His exception from judgment. For instance, the prophet Daniel urged his friends at a crucial moment in their lives, *"...to plead for mercy from the God of heaven concerning this mystery..."* (Dan. 2:18). As a result of the pleading, God revealed the mystery to Daniel the prophet in a vision, and that revelation saved their lives from the evil schemes of a pompous king.

God's response to Daniel's prayers in the Book of Daniel chapter 10 illustrates the dynamics of the principle of sending our spoken words into the heavenlies when we handle our earthly affairs, *"He* [an angel] *said, 'Daniel, you who are highly esteemed, consider carefully the words I am about to speak to you, and stand up, for I have now been sent to you.' And when he said this to me, I stood up trembling. Then he continued, 'Do not be afraid, Daniel.* **Since the first day that you set your mind to gain understanding and to humble yourself before your God, your words were** *heard, and I have **come in response to them**. But the **prince of the Persian kingdom** resisted me twenty-one days. Then **Michael, one of the chief princes**, came to help me, because I was detained there with the king of Persia. Now I have come to explain to you what will happen to your people in the future, for the vision concerns a time yet to come"'* (Daniel 10:11-14).

A very direct way of approaching the heavenly realm is
by spoken words. Words can ascend as spiritual
arrows into the heavenly places.

We know that the words of a righteous person avail much and are capable of ascending unto the heavenlies, as the angelic messenger told Daniel in the previous passage. Jesus says the words He speaks are spirits and that they have life (see John 6:63). And the Bible teaches that those with clean hands and those who harbor no iniquity in their hearts, God will hear when they pray—their words are capable of ascending unto the holy hills of God. As we cannot ascend with our earthen bodies, we ascend in the spirit commonly by sending words to the heavenlies.

> *Who may ascend the hill of the Lord? Who may stand in his holy place? He who has **clean hands and a pure heart**, who does not lift up his soul to an idol or swear by what is false. **He will receive blessing from the Lord and vindication from God** his Saviour. Such is the generation of those who seek him, who seek your face, O God of Jacob. Selah* (Psalm 24:3-6).

A PURE HEART AND CLEAN HANDS

Come and listen, all you who fear God; let me tell you what He has done for me. I cried out to Him with my mouth; His praise was on my tongue. If I had cherished sin in my heart, the Lord would not have listened; but God has surely listened and heard my voice in prayer. Praise be to God, who has not rejected my prayer or withheld His love from me! (Psalm 66:16-20)

The emphasis here is the role of a pure heart in determining how far our spoken word can go. A pure heart clears the way for our word to ascend to the heavenlies and reach God. The purity of your heart determines your relationship with the Father in heaven and the ability to contend with the spiritual forces of evil in heavenly realm. This also is evident from what the angel messenger said to Daniel: *"Daniel, you who are highly esteemed, consider carefully the words I am about to speak to you, and stand up, for I have now been sent to you." And when he said this to me, I stood up trembling"* (Dan. 10:11).

The Bible also says, *"Blessed are the pure in heart, for they will **see** God"* (Matt. 5:8).

The word *see* symbolizes, among other meanings, divine enlightenment or understanding to gain insightful knowledge of something, it also implies this process is predicated on the child-like purity of the heart.

Jesus also said, *"Let the little children come to me, and do not hinder them, for the kingdom of God belongs to such as these. I tell you the truth, anyone who will not receive the kingdom of God like a little child will never enter it"* (Mark 10:14-15).

The word *children* here also metaphorically refers to a state of innocence and the child-like purity of the heart that is required before the presence of Jesus Christ and to possess the Kingdom of God:

*Who may ascend the hill of the Lord? Who may stand in his holy place? He who has **clean hands and a pure heart**...* (Psalm 24:3-4).

In accordance with Psalm 24, the words of a person with clean hands can ascend the holy hills of God as spiritual arrows and obtain justice (vindication) and blessing (enablement) from God. You can not ascend with your earthly body. The ability of spoken words to ascend into the heavens is therefore closely related to the person's right standing with God. The implication is that with right standing with God, **our words can ascend into the heavenly realm and bring justice for us from the heavenly court sessions.**

In the Old Testament, God symbolized the need for clean hands before coming into His presence especially for the priests, but the same is true for us spiritually. This is what the Bible says:

> *He then made ten basins for washing and placed five on the south side and five on the north. In them the things to be used for the burnt offerings were rinsed, but the Sea was to be used by the priests for washing* (2 Chronicles 4:6).

> *Make a bronze basin, with its bronze stand, for washing. Place it between the Tent of Meeting and the altar and put water in it. Aaron and his sons are to wash their hands and feet with water from it. Whenever they enter the Tent of Meeting, they shall wash with water so that they will not die. Also, when they approach the altar to minister by presenting an offering made to the Lord by fire, they shall wash their hands and feet so that they will not die. This is to be a lasting ordinance for Aaron and his descendants for the generations to come* (Exodus 30:18-21).

This is how King Hezekiah put action to the words of Psalm 24. The good side of King Hezekiah's life reflects the principles of Psalm 24. He trusted in the Lord, the God of Israel: *"Hezekiah trusted in the Lord, the God of Israel. There was no one like him among all the kings of Judah, either before him or after him. He held fast to the Lord and did not cease to follow him; he kept the commands the Lord had given Moses"* (2 Kings 18:5-6).

He cleansed Judah from idol worshiping: *"He did what was right in the eyes of the Lord, just as his father David had done. He removed the high places, smashed the sacred stones and cut down the Asherah poles. He broke into pieces the bronze snake Moses had made, for up to that time the Israelites had been burning incense to it. (It was called Nehushtan)"* (2 Kings 18:3-4).

He cut off national ties with evil nations around Judah: *"And the Lord was with him; he was successful in whatever he undertook. He rebelled against the king of Assyria and did not serve him. From watchtower to fortified city, he defeated the Philistines, as far as Gaza and its territory"* (2 Kings 18:7-8).

And when he prayed about his illness, he was healed and granted dramatic and unprecedented extension of his life. When the prophet Isaiah brought the news of impending death to King Hezekiah, the king appealed to God and the verdict was reversed:

> *In those days Hezekiah became ill and was at the point of death. The prophet Isaiah son of Amoz went to him and said, "This is what the Lord says: 'Put your house in order, because you are going to die; you will not recover.' Hezekiah turned his face to the wall and prayed to the Lord, "Remember, O Lord, how I have walked before you faithfully and with wholehearted devotion and have done what is good in your eyes." And Hezekiah wept bitterly. Before Isaiah had left the middle court, the word of the Lord came to him: "Go back and tell Hezekiah, the leader of my people, 'This is what the Lord, the God of your father David, says: I have heard your prayer and seen your tears; I will heal you. On the third day from now you will go up to the temple of the Lord. I will add fifteen years to your life. And I will deliver you and this city from the hand of the king of Assyria. I will defend this city for my sake and for the sake of my servant David'"* (2 Kings 20:1-6).

King Hezekiah stands out in the Old Testament as one whose prayers were often answered and often in the most dramatic way. We can see this from the previous Scripture passage as well as in the following passage:

> *Although most of the many people who came from Ephraim, Manasseh, Issachar and Zebulun had not purified themselves, yet they ate the Passover, contrary to what was written. But Hezekiah prayed for them, saying, "May the Lord, who is good, pardon everyone who sets his heart on seeking God—the Lord, the God of his fathers—even if he is not clean according to the rules of the sanctuary." And the Lord heard Hezekiah and healed the people* (2 Chronicles 30:18-20).

King Hezekiah brought justice to the injustice perpetuated by the evil King Sennacherib by appealing to heavenly justice:

Hezekiah received the letter from the messengers and read it. Then he went up to the temple of the Lord and spread it out before the Lord. And Hezekiah prayed to the Lord: "O Lord, God of Israel, enthroned between the cherubim, You alone are God over all the kingdoms of the earth. You have made heaven and earth. Give ear, O Lord, and hear; open your eyes, O Lord, and see; listen to the words Sennacherib has sent to insult the living God. It is true, O Lord, that the Assyrian kings have laid waste these nations and their lands. They have thrown their gods into the fire and destroyed them, for they were not gods but only wood and stone, fashioned by men's hands. Now, O Lord our God, deliver us from his hand, so that all kingdoms on earth may know that You alone, O Lord, are God" (2 Kings 19:14-19).

WALKING IN HUMILITY

When I shut up the heavens so that there is no rain, or command locusts to devour the land or send a plague among My people, if My people, who are called by My name, will humble themselves and pray and seek My face and turn from their wicked ways, then will I hear from heaven and will forgive their sin and will heal their land. Now My eyes will be open and My ears attentive to the prayers offered in this place (2 Chronicles 7:13-15).

Four basic requirements mentioned as necessary for God to hear our petition in heaven are: humility, prayers, seeking the face of God, and turning away from evil. With these requirements in place, our prayers will penetrate the heavenlies and reach God. God is guaranteed to respond to such prayers by: hearing in heaven, forgiving our sins, healing the land, and turning His eyes and ears toward us.

King David lived a life of humility and of continuous repentance. He was described as a man after God's own heart. The Scripture is full of instances when David sought the face and counsel of God on issues that came across his path in life. David once prayed, *"It is a broken spirit you want—remorse and penitence. A broken and contrite heart, O God you will not ignore!"* (Ps. 51:17 TLB).

Another example of words ascending into the heavenly realm as spiritual arrows is recorded in the story of Ahithophel and how God frustrated his counsel against David.

Let's look at Ahithophel's story in close detail. Ahithophel was a privy counsellor to King David, and of his counsel, the Bible records: *"Absalom did whatever Ahithophel told him to, just as David had, for every word Ahithophel spoke seemed as **wise as though it had come directly from the mouth of God"** (2 Sam. 16:23 TLB).

Bathsheba was the granddaughter of Ahithophel; *"One evening David got up from his bed and walked around on the roof of the palace. From the roof he saw a woman bathing. The woman was very beautiful, and David sent someone to find out about her. The man said, "Isn't this Bathsheba, **the daughter of Eliam** and the wife of Uriah the Hittite?"* (2 Sam. 11:2-3). *Eliphelet son of Ahasbai the Maacathite, **Eliam son of Ahithophel** the Gilonite* (2 Sam. 23:34).

Out of an unforgiving heart because of David's adulterous relation with Bathsheba, Anithophel joined Absalom's rebellion against David. When David heard that his trusted counselor, Ahithophel, had joined Absalom's conspiracy, he was upset and issued a decree against the potential counsel that Ahithophel may give Absalom.

> *Now David had been told, "Ahithophel is among the conspirators with Absalom." So David prayed, "O Lord, turn Ahithophel's counsel into foolishness"* (2 Samuel 15:31).

I believe David's words were heard in heaven and Ahithophel's good counsel to Absalom was judged and frustrated by God: *"Absalom and all the men of Israel said, 'The advice of Hushai the Arkite is better than that of Ahithophel.' **For the Lord had determined to frustrate the good advice of Ahithophel** in order to bring disaster on Absalom"* (2 Sam. 17:14).

Other ways to access the heavenly realms include inputting and influencing the happenings in the heavenly realm via the prophetic privilege of intercession. Prophetic privilege of intercession is the art of using the privilege of a revelation as the platform for interceding for what is revealed. However, this by implication involves operating in prophetic anointing or in the spirit of prophecy (the testimony of Jesus).

> *He and all his family were devout and God-fearing; he gave generously to those in need and prayed to God regularly. One day at about three in the afternoon he had a vision. He distinctly saw an angel of God, who came to him and said, "Cornelius!" Cornelius stared at him in fear. "What is it, Lord?" he asked. The angel answered, "Your prayers and gifts to the poor have come up as a memorial offering before God (Acts 10:2-4).*

DECLARATIONS

"Thou shalt also decree a thing, and it shall be established unto thee..." (Job 22:28 KJV).

1. May the mercy of God abound toward me and open up the heaven over my head that I might receive revelations from God. O God, may You bring unity between my friends and me so we may plead with You on behalf of each other and also for the welfare of others.

    "He urged them to plead for mercy from the God of heaven concerning the mystery" (Daniel 2:18).

2. O God, grant me holy hands that will be acceptable unto You so my words can ascend onto the hills of God and my cries to You will be heard.

    "...Do not be afraid, Daniel. Since the first day that you set your mind to gain understanding and to humble yourself before your God, your words were heard, and I have come in response to them" (Daniel 10:12).

"So I have come down to rescue them from the hand of the Egyptians and to bring them up out of that land into a good and spacious land, a land flowing with milk and honey—the home of the Canaanites, Hittites, Amorites, Perizzites, Hivites and Jebusites. And now the cry of the Israelites has reached me, and I have seen the way the Egyptians are oppressing them. So now, go. I am sending you to Pharaoh to bring my people the Israelites out of Egypt" (Exodus 3:8-10).

"Who may ascend the hill of the Lord? Who may stand in his holy place? He who has clean hands and a pure heart, who does not lift up his soul to an idol or swear by what is false" (Psalm 24:3-4).

3. O God, turn every accusation and malicious statement coming against me into foolishness. May they not prosper.

    "Now David had been told, 'Ahithophel is among the conspirators with Absalom.' So David prayed, 'O Lord, turn Ahithophel's counsel into foolishness'" (2 Samuel 15:31).

4. *"Help me, Lord, to make the meditations of my heart and the words of my mouth be acceptable unto you, God. Purify my mouth and back up the words that I speak"* (Proverbs 12:18).

    "Reckless words pierce like a sword, but the tongue of the wise brings healing" (Proverbs 12:18).

    "He who guards his mouth and his tongue keeps himself from calamity" (Proverbs 21:23).

    "The tongue has the power of life and death, and those who love it will eat its fruit" (Proverbs 18:21).

    "The tongue that brings healing is a tree of life, but a deceitful tongue crushes the spirit" (Proverbs 15:4).

"The Sovereign Lord has given me an instructed tongue, to know the word that sustains the weary. He wakens me morning by morning, wakens my ear to listen like one being taught" (Isaiah 50:4).

5. May the name of the Lord grant me victory and may God contend with those who contend with me. God has given weapons that are more powerful than the weapons of this world and I shall demolish every argument or stronghold that sets itself over the knowledge of Christ Jesus.

David said to the Philistine, "You come against me with sword and spear and javelin, but I come against you in the name of the Lord Almighty, the God of the armies of Israel, whom you have defied. This day the Lord will hand you over to me, and I'll strike you down and cut off your head. Today I will give the carcasses of the Philistine army to the birds of the air and the beasts of the earth, and the whole world will know that there is a God in Israel" (1 Samuel 17:45-46).

"Contend, O Lord, with those who contend with me; fight against those who fight against me. Take up shield and buckler; arise and come to my aid. Brandish spear and javelin against those who pursue me. Say to my soul, 'I am your salvation'" (Psalm 35:1-3).

"For though we live in the world, we do not wage war as the world does. The weapons we fight with are not the weapons of the world. On the contrary, they have divine power to demolish strongholds. We demolish arguments and every pretension that sets itself up against the knowledge of God, and we take captive every thought to make it obedient to Christ" (2 Corinthians 10:3-5).

Chapter 5

THE POWER OF THE SPOKEN WORD

THE BIBLE SAYS, *"By faith we understand that the worlds were framed by the word of God so that the things which are seen were not made of things which are visible"* (Heb. 11:3 NKJV). The most common and often the easiest way to influence and make things out of the invisible is by the power of spoken words! However, spoken words come in various levels of strength and in different ways. Spoken words are like spiritual arrows into the unseen world and can bring good or harmful consequences upon humankind in the natural world. The words you speak can rescue you in times of trouble *"The words of the wicked lie in wait for blood, but the speech of the upright rescues them"* (Prov. 12:6). This chapter discusses why some spoken words are more effective than others.

THE SPOKEN WORD

The power of spoken words and the power of the mouth are important in the grace to administer the justice of God on earth. Words transmit images, and imagery is important in breaking the inertia of dormant promises activating them into motion toward fulfillment. An image is something that can be pictured, and images stimulate and propel human imagination and the power of conceptualization. Spoken words are seeds that can be sowed in the spiritual realm. And they are also the building blocks of the imagery in the mind of a hearer.

Spoken words are like spiritual arrows into the unseen world.

Once a word is sown and nurtured, it will eventually germinate and mature into fruition, regardless of whether it was a good seed or a bad seed. That is why the Bible says, *"The sower sows the word"* (Mark 4:14), all of us are sowing seeds of spoken words every time we speak. In effect, words control the world. That being true, often the enemy will try to shoot wrong thoughts into our minds so as to get us to speak them. Particularly when they are negative, he sits back to watch as we reap what we say. The lives that most people live today are the result of what they said yesterday. What we say can trigger off things in the hands of the devil and his system—or in the hands of the Almighty God and His Kingdom agents. The Bible says, *"The tongue has the power of life and death, and those who love it will eat its fruit"* (Prov. 18:21). In other words, the tongue can become the power of life if we cooperate with God or power of death if we cooperate with the devil. No wonder the Psalmist pleaded with God in Psalm 141:3. *"Set a guard over my mouth, O Lord; keep watch over the door of my lips."* In a sobering reminder God said, *"So tell them, as surely as I live, declares the Lord, I will do to you the very things I heard you say"* (Num. 14:28). What have you been saying lately?

Even angels are activated to act on our behalf by the words of our mouth: *"angels... harken to the voice of His word"* (Ps. 103:20). Spoken word is the means by which we give voice to the word of God on earth, and angels are great instruments of justice in the hands of God—what we say or don't say can hinder or activate angels meant to minister to us.

The universe was created by the spoken word of God. Satan copied this and deceived Eve by the power of his spoken word. But God so loved the world that He sent His begotten son to die for us (see John 3:16). God's Son, who is the Word of God, became flesh and dwelt among us. In actuality, Jesus Christ is the logo word!

Even the rhema word—the word in season—is also by the Spirit of Christ. Truly as the Bible says, Jesus Christ the Word of God "made flesh" came into the world to destroy the work of the enemy—the satanic spoken word sowed in the Garden of Eden.

Words transmit images, and imagery is important in breaking the inertia of dormant promises activating them into motion toward fulfillment.

You begin to see that the fall of man and the redemptive power of the blood of Jesus Christ centers on the battle of the spoken word of satan being destroyed by the Word of God spoken on our behalf. It is through the redemptive power of the blood of Jesus Christ that humankind is "potentially" restored to God. I use the word potentially because the actuality depends on each individual allowing the finished work of the cross to apply to them on a personal basis. As the Scriptures say, we also need to speak forth the word, *"let the redeemed of the Lord say so."* So "to be or not to be" often boils down to the battle of spoken words!

Accessing, releasing, and obtaining our promises from the heavenly realm is connected with the power of spoken words. In the Book of Daniel, the Bible records that an angelic message was released from heaven at the words that Daniel spoke:

> He [an angel] *said, "Daniel, you who are highly esteemed, consider carefully the words I am about to speak to you, and stand up, for I have now been sent to you." And when he said this to me, I stood up trembling. Then he continued, "Do not be afraid, Daniel. Since the first day that you set your mind to gain understanding and to humble yourself before your God, your words were heard, and I have come in response to them. But the prince of the Persian kingdom resisted me twenty-one days. Then Michael, one of the chief princes, came to help me, because I was detained there with the king of Persia. Now I have*

come to explain to you what will happen to your people in the future, for the vision concerns a time yet to come" (Daniel 10:11-14).

Words have the power of dynamite that can make or break, or sometimes even destroy a people. Even truthful words can cause hurts unless properly cushioned with wisdom. Words are so powerful that they mean the difference between life and death and can save a person or a nation.

Words have the power of dynamite.

The power of the spoken word and the mouth are quite easily noticeable by the influence they exert on the lives of people in the natural world. Sometimes at the most difficult and uncertain times, a single voice can give the clear and unambiguous course of action and stir the people in the right or wrong direction. The prophet Haggai was one of the most successful prophets in the whole of the Bible. His message was one of the shortest messages in the Bible, yet the words he spoke rang clear in a time of Israel's trouble and confusion:

> *Then Zerubbabel son of Shealtiel, Joshua son of Jehozadak, the high priest,* ***and the whole remnant of the people obeyed the voice of the Lord their God and the message of the prophet Haggai,*** *because the Lord their God had sent him. And the people feared the Lord* (Haggai 1:12).

Many people believe that it was through the power of the spoken word that Prime Minister Winston Churchill saved Britain in World War II. Equally significant was the spoken words of civil rights leader Martin Luther King Jr. that captured America's conscience in the 1950s. This weight of the spoken words of Martin Luther King Jr. played a prominent role that led to one of the greatest national reawakenings in the United States of America. More recently we have seen how the power of spoken words played a key role in electing the first African American to the presidency of the United States. No one could ignore the oratory power of President Barack Obama in the 2008 general election. These examples illustrate how spoken words brought visible and tangible changes in the realm of the physical. The power of the spoken word is even more so in the spirit realm.

YOUR MOUTH AND YOUR WORDS

However, the power and influence of spoken words and indeed of the mouth itself have great significance in the supernatural realm. In Bible days, the prophet Jeremiah was given a mammoth task. God chose him to be a prophet to an obstinate nation that would not listen to him. His only one resource was his mouth: *"Then the Lord reached out his hand and touched my mouth and said to me, "Now, I have put **My words in your mouth**. See, today I appoint you over nations and kingdoms to uproot and tear down, to destroy and overthrow, to build and to plant"* (Jer. 1:9-10).

Later, still emphasizing the significance of the power of spoken word, God said to Jeremiah, *"...Because the people have spoken these words, I will make **My words in your mouth a fire** and these people the wood it consumes"* (Jer. 5:14).

At the commissioning of Moses to deliver the Israelites from Egypt, Moses complained that he was not eloquent in speech, but God introduced the concept of associating the mouth and the spoken word and He simply reminded Moses that He made the mouth from which words are spoken:

> *Moses said to the Lord, "O Lord, I have never been eloquent, neither in the past nor since you have spoken to your servant. I am slow of speech and tongue." The Lord said to him, "Who gave man his mouth? Who makes him deaf or mute? Who gives him sight or makes him blind? Is it not I, the Lord? Now go; I will help you speak and will teach you what to say"* (Exodus 4:10-12).

God further reiterated the significance of the associating power of the spoken words with the state of the mouth from which they come: *"As for Me, this is My covenant with them* [His people], *says the Lord 'My Spirit, who is on you and My words that I have put in your mouth will not depart from your mouth or from the mouths of your children or from the mouths of their descendants, from this time on and forever,' says the Lord"* (Isa. 59:21).

Also, in an earlier chapter of the Book of Isaiah, the prophet said, *"He made **my mouth like a sharpened sword,** in the shadow of His hand he Hid me; He made me into a polished arrow and concealed me in His quiver. He said to me, 'You are My servant, Israel, in whom I will display My splendor'"* (Isa. 49:2-3).

Speaking of God Himself, the Psalmist said, *"By the word of the Lord were the heavens made, their starry host by the breath of His mouth"* (Ps. 33:6). Such is the significance of the mouth and the power of the words that come from the mouth.

It is clear that the effectiveness of the spoken word is related to the state of the mouth from which the word is spoken. It is perhaps a sober thought to know that you are responsible for the state of your mouth. You should endeavor to sanctify your tongue by putting *"away perversity from your mouth; keep corrupt talk far from your lips"* (Prov. 4:24). That is why in the Book of Ephesians 4:29-30, apostle Paul admonished us, *"let no corrupt communication proceed out of your mouth but that which is good to use of edifying, that it may minister grace unto others"* (KJV). Apostle James was very stern on the subject of the state of the mouth and the power of spoken words:

> *Out of the same mouth come praise and cursing. My brothers, this should not be* (James 3:10).

GIVE VOICE TO THE WORD OF GOD

In the words of the Psalmist, *"The Lord announced the word, and great was the company of those who proclaimed it"* (Ps. 68:11). Greatness will undoubtedly follow those who give voice to the words of God (proclamation of the words of God). The Bible says; *"Let the redeemed of the Lord say this—those He redeemed from the hand of the foe"* (Ps. 107:2). Such is the degree of emphasis that God places on the significance of the word that is spoken and which should be differentiated from the one that remains only at the thought stage in the mind (the unspoken word).

Speaking on this subject, God said to Joshua, *"Do not let this Book of the Law depart from **your mouth**; meditate on it day and night, so that you may be careful to do everything written in it. Then you will be prosperous and successful"* (Josh.

1:8). God made it clear that it is the word in Joshua's mouth that will produce results for him because that is the one that eventually is spoken. Perhaps this is why in the first chapter of the Book of Genesis, in the process of creation of the earth, the Bible records that God spoke on several occasions. God Himself spoke the entire creation into being.

Jesus Christ in His teaching, reminded us that if we have faith and then speak out, that mountains will move at our spoken words: *"I tell you the truth, if anyone says to this mountain, 'Go, throw yourself into the sea,' and does not doubt in his heart but believes that what he says will happen, it will be done for him"* (Mark 11:23).

To two of the outstanding prophets in the Old Testament, Jeremiah and Isaiah, God said; *"I put My word in your mouth." "I have put My words in your mouth and covered you with the shadow of My hand—I who set the heavens in place, who laid the foundations of the earth, and who say to Zion, 'You are My people'"* (Isa. 51:16). Therefore their calling and ministries were intimately connected with the power of the words that came from their mouths.

In general, the words in the mouth are so important that every one of us will eventually be judged by them: *"...I [God] will judge you by your own words..."* (Luke 19:22).

Spoken Words as Living Exhibits

In the Book of Micah, spoken words were to serve as living exhibits in both the physical and the heavenly realm:

> *...Stand up, plead your case before the mountain, let the hills hear what you have to say. Hear, O mountains, the Lord's accusations, listen, you everlasting foundation of the earth. For the Lord has case against His people. He is lodging a charge against Israel* (Micah 6:1-2).

Spoken Words as Spiritual Arrows

The Bible says in Psalms 64:3, *"They sharpen their tongues like swords and aim their words like deadly arrows."* Here the psalmist likens spoken words to spiritual arrows! Regarding the significance of spoken words, Jesus Christ also admonished us that, *"The Spirit gives life; the flesh counts for nothing. The words I have spoken to you are spirit and they are life"* (John 6:63).

Spoken words are spirit and therefore they are invisible and operate in a way you may not be able to see, but they can have lasting effects. Spirits don't die. Also, spoken words have life. They are made of spiritual substance and can perpetuate and maintain themselves either in dormant or active forms.

Spoken words are also like packages. Spoken words as packages can exist in dormant or active forms. A spoken word that is dormant is a word that exists only in the spirit realm waiting for the right condition to manifest in the natural realm or to be fulfilled in the natural realm. It is our responsibility to activate the dormant words of blessings over our lives. One of the ways we can do this is to ensure we comply with the divine requirement for it to be fulfilled and then to speak it into being.

It is by spoken words that blessings or inheritance are conferred on a person or on a generation. God spoke blessing on Abraham and Abraham spoke the blessing on Isaac. Isaac blessed Jacob by the power of the spoken word. Jacob also blessed his children with spoken words.

**Spoken words as packages
can exist in dormant or active forms.**

Our words can bring immediate response from the throne of God, as the angel told the prophet Daniel that his words triggered response in heaven on the very day he spoke them. *"Then he continued, 'Do not be afraid, Daniel. Since the first day that you set your mind to gain understanding and to humble yourself before your God, your words were heard, and I have come in response to them'"* (Dan. 10:12). The Psalmist says, *"May the words of my mouth and the meditation of my heart be pleasing in Your sight, O Lord, my Rock and my Redeemer"* (Ps. 19:14).

The Spoken Word of God

God said in Isaiah 55:10-11, *"As the rain and snow come down from heaven...so is My word that goes out from My mouth but will accomplish what I desire and achieve the purpose for which I sent it."* Hebrews 4:12 in the Amplified Bible says, *"For the word God speaks is alive and full of power [making it active, operative, energizing, and effective]; it is sharper than two-edged sword, penetrating to the dividing line of the breath of life (soul) and [the immortal] spirit, and of joints and marrow [of the deepest parts of our nature], exposing and sifting and judging the very thoughts and purpose of the heart."*

The spoken word of God can convey multiple meanings as the Psalmist reminds us, *"One thing God has spoken, two things have I heard: that You, O God, are strong"* (Ps. 62:11). This is because God speaks with great economy of words.

Referring to the power behind God's spoken words, the Lord Himself asks this question, *"Is not my word like fire,"* declares the Lord, *"and like a hammer that breaks a rock in pieces?"* (Jer. 23:29).

Even the heavens were made at the spoken words of God: *"By the word of the Lord were the heavens made, their starry host by the breath of His mouth"* (Ps. 33:6).

The word of God has enough spiritual substance to bring health to our body *"for they are life to those who find them and health to a man's whole body"* (Prov. 4:22).

Even the *sound* of the voice of God is awesome:

> *The voice of the Lord is over the waters; the God of glory thunders, the Lord thunders over the mighty waters. The voice of the Lord is power-ful; the voice of the Lord is majestic. The voice of the Lord breaks the cedars; the Lord breaks in pieces the cedars of Lebanon. He makes Lebanon skip like a calf, Sirion like a young wild ox. The voice of the Lord strikes with flashes of lightning. The voice of the Lord shakes the desert; the Lord shakes the Desert of Kadesh. The voice of the Lord twists the oaks and strips the forests bare. And in His temple all cry, "Glory!"* (Psalm 29:3-9)

This is why you imbed the qualities of God in every spiritual encounter you have with Him. As you receive regular spiritual encounters with God, you gradually imbed the nature of God and attain a heightened level of spirituality within yourself.

The deadly words of satan are also spirits:

> *Then I saw three evil spirits that looked like frogs; they came out of the mouth of the dragon, out of the mouth of the beast and out of the mouth of the false prophet. They are spirits of demons performing miraculous signs, and they go out to the kings of the whole world, to gather them for the battle on the great day of God Almighty* (Revelation 16:13-14).

This is why the mere words from the wife of King Ahab, Jezebel, were sufficient to drive a powerful prophet like Elijah into a state of depression and almost to a point of suicide.

The effective power behind the spoken word depends on several things:

- The speaker's right standing with God.
- The faith with which it is said. Note that the power of the spoken word of the devil is often related to how much fear it generates in man.
- The state of the mouth of the speaker; perverse lips produce death, and righteous lips produce life.
- Was the word said inspired by God and is it birthed in the Holy Spirit? When the heart overflows the mouth speaks.
- Is what was said in line with the plans of God? No wisdom, no plans could work against that of God.
- The speaker's authority over the situation. Most of the power of the devil is derived on this premise: any sin in our lives that gives the devil a landing pad in our situation makes the power of the devil more effective.
- The battle of spoken words can be easily seen when compared side by side:

GODLY WAY	EVIL WAY
By spoken words the heavens and the earth were created.	By spoken words satan deceived Eve to disobey God. Man and creation fell.
Genesis 1	Genesis 3
To redeem man and the fallen creation, the Word became flesh and dwelt among us.	Satan could not counterfeit this. Satan is not a creator.
John 1:14	
Jesus Christ said that the words He spoke are spirit and are life.	Satan's words are also spirit but bring only death.
John 6:63	Proverbs 12:6
	Revelation 16:13-14
The tongue of man has the power of life and death.	Satan can make a man say things that are detrimental to himself.
Proverbs 18:21	Proverbs 18:21
Let the redeemed of the Lord say so.	Do not yield yourself as a mouth piece for the devil, like Job's wife.
The true prophet of God declares by the spoken word.	The false prophet, Jezebel, declares by spoken words.
1 Kings 17:1	1 Kings 19:1
The final victory of the mouth and word.	
Revelation 19:15-16	

DECLARATIONS

"Thou shalt also decree a thing, and it shall be established unto thee..." (Job 22:28 KJV).

1. The Lord has purified my tongue and has placed the power of life and death on my tongue. My word shall be like fire and hammer to the enemy and his plans. The power in my tongue shall cancel all evil pronouncements that may come against me.

   "Then the Lord reached out His hand and touched my mouth and said to me, "Now, I have put My words in your mouth. See, today I appoint you over nations and kingdoms to uproot and tear down, to destroy and overthrow, to build and to plant" (Jeremiah 1:9-10).

   "The tongue has the power of life and death, and those who love it will eat its fruit" (Proverbs 18:21).

   "The tongue that brings healing is a tree of life, but a deceitful tongue crushes the spirit" (Proverbs 15:4).

   "The Sovereign Lord has given me an instructed tongue, to know the word that sustains the weary. He wakens me morning by morning, wakens my ear to listen like one being taught" (Isaiah 50:4).

   "Is not my word like fire," declares the Lord, "and like a hammer that breaks a rock in pieces?" (Jeremiah 23:29).

2. The Lord is my salvation and my help in time of trouble and I shall not be overcome by evil.

   "All the nations surrounded me, but in the name of the Lord I cut them off. They surrounded me on every side, but in the name of the Lord I cut them off. They swarmed around me like bees, but they died out as quickly as burning thorns; in the name of the Lord I cut them off. I was pushed back and about to fall, but the Lord helped me. The Lord is my strength and my song; He has become my salvation" (Psalm 118:10-14).

Chapter 6

PROCLAMATIONS, DECREES, AND EDICTS

IN ORDER TO BRING divine justice to the earth, God has decrees, pronouncements, or commandments that are instituted to regulate human behavior to ensure the strict standards of wrongs and rights and a code of conduct that applies to everyone. On the other hand, the devil and his agents also have decrees or pronouncements targeted to push people out of God's plan for them and to bring about chaos and confusion: *"The words of the wicked are like a murderous ambush"* (Prov. 12:6 NLT). How these two systems of verbal pronouncements play out in the realities of our lives is the subject of this part of our discussion.

As we pass through life, not only do *things* get attached to us but also *words*. Words, as invisible spiritual arrows either from the earth or from the heavenly realm, get targeted at us. These words often carry significant spiritual power that need to be rightly handled to avoid any harmful consequences or channeled to achieve righteous benefits.

DECLARATION

To verbalize a word is called *declaration*. An idea or a word or concept in our minds needs to be verbalized to become a declaration. A declaration, whether done privately or publicly, has the power to activate a dormant promise or curse into kinetic motion of fulfillment. So declaration is the easiest and often the first step toward fulfillment of a promise. Declaration from the righteous can often be sufficient to counter the evil intentions of the devil and his agents.

To verbalize a word is called *declaration*.

PROCLAMATION

On the other hand, a declaration done publicly is known as *proclamation*. Therefore, to proclaim is to announce something publicly. You cannot proclaim something privately because proclamation requires public witnessing. And because of the evidence of a witness, it has a superior power than a declaration. Usually the public declaration (proclamation) has both spiritual invisible and natural visible witnesses. Because of this, it can be quite powerful as well as being much more difficult to counter if emanating from the devil or his agents.

A declaration done publicly is known as *proclamation*.

The significance of witnesses can be seen in the following proclamations:

- As the Israelites crossed between the Ebal and Gezirim mountains and walked along the historical valley where Abraham was believed to have first worshiped God after receiving the original promise of the land in Genesis 15, they hear the resounding proclamations of curses on one mountain and blessings on the other mountain. They hear the power of contradictions and the paradoxes of life. If they obey God, blessing will be bestowed on them and if they choose to disobey Him, curses will come upon them. This enactment was a profoundly symbolic event for the Israelites. From the tops of the two mountains, the great expanse of the Promised Land could be seen. Far more than that, these words of pronouncement were not only mere words echoed by the leaders, these pronouncements were also reminders to the spirit world that the Israelites have put in place established ordinances that will govern their behavior in the Promised Land. The words also exhibit in the unseen world because spoken words are spirits and the mountains on which they were declared serve as witnesses in the physical world to the proclamations.

- Also, God spoke to the land as a witness when He cursed Jehoiachin, king of Judah: *"O land, land, land, **hear the word of the Lord!** This is what the Lord says: "Record this man as if childless, a man who will not prosper in his lifetime, for none of his offspring will prosper, none will sit on the throne of David or rule anymore in Judah"* (Jer. 22:29-30).

- God said to Cain that the blood of Abel cried out to Him from the ground which was a witness to his awful sin. In many other instances, nature bears witness to what we say or do in this world: *"Stand up, plead your case **before the mountain, let the hills hear what you have to say. Hear, O mountains,** the Lord's accusations, listen you everlasting foundation of the earth. For the Lord has case against His people. He is lodging a charge...* (Micah 6:1-2).

- In the Book of Ecclesiastes, the Bible warns that even angels are witnesses to our proclamations on earth: *"Do not let your mouth lead you into sin. And do not protest to the temple messenger, 'My vow was a mistake.' Why should God be angry at what you say and destroy the work of your hands?"* (Ecclesiastes 5:6)

DECREE

A proclamation becomes a *decree* if it carries a form of authoritative power behind it. The power behind any verbal package is related to the spiritual standing of the source or person pronouncing the word. The blood of Abel speaks and the blood of Jesus also speaks, but the Bible says that the pronouncement of the blood of Jesus speaks better things than that of the blood of Abel. Decrees from God are much more powerful than the decrees from satan or his agents.

A decree is an authoritative order that has the force of law behind it. Therefore a decree can come in any of the following formats: a ruling, an announcement, a declaration, a verdict, a judgment, an order, or a pronouncement. Decrees have varying levels of authority and power behind them. So anybody can issue a decree provided he or she has some authority to back it up. For instance, the head of the home can issue decrees for the household.

A proclamation becomes a *decree* if it carries a form of authoritative power behind it.

We have to fulfill certain criteria to be able to make effective decrees:

> *Surely then you will find delight in the Almighty and will lift up your face to God. You will pray to Him, and He will hear you, and you will fulfill your vows. What you decide on will be done, and light will shine on your ways* (Job 22:26-28).

Notice in this Scripture passage from Job that before a *godly* decree can become powerful, the proclaimer needs to:

- Delight him or herself in Almighty God.
- Lift up his or her face to God.
- Pray to God.
- Enter into His council and deliberate with Him.
- Fulfill his or her vows.
- Be a person of faith, not wavering.
- Be a resolute person.

When these conditions are satisfied then the Bible says, *"Thou shalt also decree a thing and it shall be established unto thee, and the light shall shine upon thy ways"* (KJV).

On the other hand, the power of *evil* decrees is predicated mainly on:

- Generating fear in the person; fear is the opposite of faith.

- The authority of the devil over the situation, that any violation of the commandments of God aids the effectiveness of evil decrees.

If a decree is not in consonance with God's will, it will be annulled or at the very least frustrated by God.

The power behind any verbal package is related to the spiritual standing of the source or person pronouncing the word.

EDICT—A SPECIAL FORM OF DECREE

However, when more recognizable authority in an area or locality backs up a decree, such as a legally binding command from a recognizable source, it becomes an *edict*. The key point is that an edict is a decree that has a recognizable source of official backing. Consequently, edicts from an evil spiritual authority are harder to resist or nullify than ordinary decrees because they are associated with the evil power of the official backing that would need to be dealt with.

> *So the administrators and the satraps went as a group to the king and said: "O King Darius, live for ever! The royal administrators, prefects, satraps, advisers and governors have all agreed that the king should issue an edict and enforce the decree that anyone who prays to any god or man during the next thirty days, except to you, O king, shall be thrown into the lions' den (Daniel 6:6-7).*

Decrees and edicts are important because they can emanate from principalities or evil powers, and that would require us to act differently from how we would act if we were dealing with godly spirits.

Empty proclamations are those spoken words that are without consonance with the will of God. The Bible says *"There is no wisdom, no insight, no plan that can succeed against the Lord"* (Prov. 21:30).

THE POWER OF INDIVIDUAL PROCLAMATION

However, not all spoken words have the same power; some words carry more power than others. Some spoken words are in fact almost empty, that is they carry no significant power. Empty proclamations are words spoken that are *not in consonance with the divine order of things.*

On the other hand, some proclamations are very powerful because they are *spoken in faith* and in line with His divine will on the matter. Spoken words derive even more power if the person saying them has right standing with God and has authority to speak on the matter.

If we proclaim the wrong things, God and His angels can become angry with us: *"Suffer not thy mouth to cause the flesh to sin; neither say thou before the angel, that it was an error: wherefore should God be angry at thy voice and destroy the work of thine hands?"* (Eccl. 5:6 KJV).

God's role in the effectiveness of spoken words is paramount. God can annul or frustrate some spoken words if they come without the love of God and if they are pronounced against the purposes of God.

> *"Now therefore go, and **I will be with thy mouth** and teach thee what thou shalt say"* (Exodus 4:12 KJV).

> *"Who foils the signs of false prophets and makes fools of diviners, who overthrows the learning of the wise and turns it into nonsense, **who carries out the words of his servants and fulfills the predictions of his messengers,** who says of Jerusalem, 'It shall be inhabited,' of the*

towns of Judah, 'They shall be built,' and of their ruins, 'I will restore them'" (Isaiah 44:25-26).

*The Lord was with Samuel as he grew up, and **He let none of his words fall to the ground*** (1 Samuel 3:19).

Other factors that determine the power behind the spoken word include the following:

- *The spiritual standing* of the person. That is right standing with God, the words of a righteous people carry weight.
- *Faith with which the spoken word* was released. As the Bible says, *"'I believed; therefore I have spoken.' With that same spirit of faith we also believe and therefore speak"* (2 Cor. 4:13).
- *The legal right of the person* over the matter.
- Allowing the word to *be birthed in the presence of the Holy Spirit* before proclaiming it.
- *Communion with the Holy Spirit.* Words are more powerful if confirmed by the Holy Spirit.
- *Studying the word* helps to align spoken words with God's Word.
- *Sanctioned in the heavenly.* It is important to wait for the word to be sanctioned in Heaven before releasing it.

Once Jotham, the only surviving son of Gideon (Jerub-Baal) was aggrieved, and he climbed a mountain and issued a proclamation against Abimelech and the people of Shechem:

> *He went to his father's home in Ophrah and on one stone murdered his seventy brothers, the sons of Jerub-Baal. But Jotham, the youngest son of Jerub-Baal, escaped by hiding. Then all the citizens of Shechem and Beth Millo gathered beside the great tree at the pillar in Shechem to crown Abimelech king. When Jotham was told about this, he climbed up on the top of Mount Gerizim and shouted to them, "Listen to me, citizens of Shechem, so that God may listen to you"* (Judges 9:5-7).

Now if you have acted honorably and in good faith when you made Abimelech king, and if you have been fair to Jerub-Baal and his family, and if you have treated him as he deserves—and to think that my father fought for you, risked his life to rescue you from the hand of Midian (but today you have revolted against my father's family, murdered his seventy sons on a single stone, and made Abimelech, the son of his slave girl, king over the citizens of Shechem because he is your brother)—if then you have acted honorably and in good faith toward Jerub-Baal and his family today, may Abimelech be your joy, and may you be his, too! But if you have not, let fire come out from Abimelech and consume you, citizens of Shechem and Beth Millo, and let fire come out from you, citizens of Shechem and Beth Millo, and consume Abimelech!" Then Jotham fled, escaping to Beer, and he lived there because he was afraid of his brother Abimelech (Judges 9:16-21).*

This was later fulfilled:

Thus God repaid the wickedness that Abimelech had done to his father by murdering his seventy brothers. God also made the men of Shechem pay for all their wickedness. The curse of Jotham son of Jerub-Baal came on them (Judges 9:56-57).

Factors that reduce the effectiveness of proclamations include the misuse of the tongue such as flattery, being abusive, saying only partial truth, an untamed tongue, and bearing false witness will weaken what a person says. Apostle James said with the same mouth you curse and with it you bless! This ought not to be so.

HOW THE POWER IN A PROCLAMATION WORKS

The power of proclamation is its capability to activate a dormant promise or simply its ability to put action to a promise. This can be achieved in a number of ways including:

- Agreement with the heavenlies, either for good or for bad.

- Activate the activities of angelic assistance on our behalf.
- Bring and realign the natural to conform to the supernatural.
- Empower the process on earth; apply action to the dormant promise.

The value of a proclamation is its inherent operative components:

- As the voice of agreement with God.
- The voice of rejection of evil decrees.
- As the means of appropriating godly promises or prophetic words.
- As the offensive weapon for shooting our words as prophetic arrows into heavenly places to scatter the devil and his cohorts.
- As a defensive weapon against the onslaught of the evil one.
- As means of voicing the word of God.
- As a means of building up faith.
- As a means of affirming God promises so we can easily remember them in times of need, like memory verses.

THE GIFT OF PROCLAMATION—A SPECIAL FORM OF ANOINTING

Every person has the power of proclamation and this is maximized if the person learns to proclaim the word of God in every situation. However, there is a special form of power of proclamation that is conferred as an anointing on a person by the Holy Spirit. This power is given specially by God to certain individuals to declare the counsel of God over a situation. This is mostly connected with those in the office of the prophet or the apostle. The Bible says that God performs the words of His servant.

The prophet Isaiah declares that God, *"carries out the words of His servants and fulfills the predictions of His messengers, who says of Jerusalem, 'It shall be inhabited,' of the towns of Judah, 'They shall be built,' and of their ruins, 'I will restore them'"* (Isa. 44:26).

The Bible said of Samuel that God never allowed his words to fall to the ground:

*"The Lord was with Samuel as he grew up, and **He let none of his words fall to the ground**"* (1 Samuel 3:19).

Like most prophets with the power of proclamation, Elijah's words were powerful and effective: *"Now Elijah the Tishbite, from Tishbe in Gilead, said to Ahab, 'As the Lord, the God of Israel, lives, whom I serve, there will be neither dew nor rain in the next few years **except at my word**"* (1 Kings 17:1). God backed up what Elijah said. And when it was time for God to send rains, God sent Elijah to announce it to Ahab the king of Israel:

> *After a long time, in the third year, the word of the Lord came to Elijah: "Go and present yourself to Ahab, and I will send rain on the land"* (1 Kings 18:1).

> *And Elijah said to Ahab, "Go, eat and drink, for there is the sound of a heavy rain"* (1 Kings 18:41).

The Book of James says,

> *Elijah was a man with a nature like ours, and he prayed earnestly that it would not rain, and it did not rain on the earth for three years and six months. Then he prayed again and the sky poured rain and the earth produced its fruit* (James 5:17-18 NASB).

God is waiting and watching over His promises (His words) to perform them, if we become the voice of proclamation on earth for His purpose as the prophet Jeremiah said, *"The word of the Lord came to me: 'What do you see, Jeremiah?' 'I see the branch of an almond tree,' I replied. The Lord said to me, 'You have seen correctly, for I am watching to see that My word is fulfilled'"* (Jer. 1:11-12).

PERSONAL TESTIMONIES

1. Before I was released to bring insights into other people's dreams (as in the interpretation of other people's dreams), I received numerous dreams in which God conferred on me the power of proclamation. On several of these encounters,

God said to me, *"I have given you the power of proclamation."* For a long time after these experiences, I did not understand the significance of them until I stepped out in faith to help others gain understanding of their dreams. In the course of doing this, it became relevant, in many instances, when it was necessary to join with the dreamer in proclaiming one of the possible options in the process of interpreting their dreams as inspired by the Holy Spirit. This was applied in the case of a dream I interpreted during a dream clinic in Seattle, Washington state, a few years ago. In this case, a certain lady had a dream in which she was involved in a car crash. In her dream, following the car crash, she saw her body crushed inside the car and all she could remember was that she saw herself floating about the place with many rescuers trying to recover her body from the wreckage. The rescuers did not notice her presence. Her immediate feeling was that she would die. I discerned what was going on in her mind, and I immediately stopped her from proclaiming her thought in my presence. The Holy Spirit had quickened me by this time that the dream was mainly symbolic. With the power of proclamation I declared to her that the dream indicated that she was coming to the end of a process in her life and she was going to begin a new process. In this new process she was going begin, she would be more Spirit-led and the transformation would amaze many people. She received this proclamation, and few years later when I met her again, she had experienced a transformation and had grown in Christ—more importantly, she lives and did not die.

2. Also I once had a dream in which the Lord asked me to send my words to an evil person that appeared in my dream encounter in order to neutralize the evil proclamation in that dream. I dreamt that a certain person came to me and mentioned that one of my children was going to experience a life-threatening illness at the age of three. When I awoke from the dream, this did not settle in my spirit. In real life, I had doubts about the prophetic standing of the person I saw in my dream. I prayed about it and drifted back to sleep again. I had another dream in which the Lord appeared to me and said "Send your words back to him." Sending my words back to the person who made the proclamation thereby disallowed the proclamation. Thank God none of my children had any trouble at the age of three, they are all well beyond the age of three.

Types of Decrees

Reversible decrees are those that can be altered by human action, usually by appealing to God:

> *This is the interpretation, O king, and this is the decree the Most High has issued against my lord the king: You will be driven away from people and will live with the wild animals; you will eat grass like cattle and be drenched with the dew of heaven. Seven times will pass by for you until you acknowledge that the Most High is sovereign over the kingdoms of men and gives them to anyone he wishes. The command to leave the stump of the tree with its roots means that your kingdom will be restored to you when you acknowledge that Heaven rules. Therefore, O king, be pleased to accept my advice: Renounce your sins by doing what is right, and your wickedness by being kind to the oppressed. It may be that then your prosperity will continue* (Daniel 4:24-27).

Irreversible decrees are those that cannot be altered by any human action. The Ten Commandments:

> *And God spoke all these words:*
>
> *"I am the Lord your God, who brought you out of Egypt, out of the land of slavery.*
>
> *"You shall have no other gods before Me.*
>
> *"You shall not make for yourself an idol in the form of anything in heaven above or on the earth beneath or in the waters below. You shall not bow down to them or worship them; for I, the Lord your God, am a jealous God, punishing the children for the sin of the fathers to the third and fourth generation of those who hate Me, but showing love to a thousand [generations] of those who love Me and keep My commandments.*
>
> *"You shall not misuse the name of the Lord your God, for the Lord will not hold anyone guiltless who misuses His name.*

PROCLAMATIONS, DECREES, AND EDICTS

"Remember the Sabbath day by keeping it holy. Six days you shall labor and do all your work, but the seventh day is a Sabbath to the Lord your God. On it you shall not do any work, neither you, nor your son or daughter, nor your manservant or maidservant, nor your animals, nor the alien within your gates..." (Exodus 20:1-17).

Mary was greatly troubled at his words and wondered what kind of greeting this might be. But the angel said to her, "Do not be afraid, Mary, you have found favor with God. You will be with child and give birth to a son, and you are to give him the name Jesus. He will be great and will be called the Son of the Most High. The Lord God will give Him the throne of his father David, and He will reign over the house of Jacob for ever; His kingdom will never end" (Luke 1:29-33).

For the Lord Himself will come down from heaven, with a loud command, with the voice of the archangel and with the trumpet call of God, and the dead in Christ will rise first. After that, we who are still alive and are left will be caught up together with them in the clouds to meet the Lord in the air. And so we will be with the Lord forever. Therefore encourage each other with these words (1 Thessalonians 4:16-18).

Powerful decrees are those that carry heavy spiritual consequences, such as the following decree:

"In the visions I saw while lying in my bed, I looked, and there before me was a messenger, a holy one, coming down from heaven. He called in a loud voice: 'Cut down the tree and trim off its branches; strip off its leaves and scatter its fruit. Let the animals flee from under it and the birds from its branches. But let the stump and its roots, bound with iron and bronze, remain in the ground, in the grass of the field. Let him be drenched with the dew of heaven, and let him live with the animals among the plants of the earth. Let his mind be changed from that of a man and let him be given the mind of an animal, till

seven times pass by for him. The decision is announced by messengers, the holy ones declare the verdict, so that the living may know that the Most High is sovereign over the kingdoms of men and gives them to anyone he wishes and sets over them the lowliest of men"' (Daniel 4:13-17).

HOW TO COUNTER AND REVERSE EVIL DECREES/EDICTS

Give the devil or his word no chance as we read in the stories of Job and the prophet Micaiah. Both of them refused to agree with the evil decrees, and so they could not alight on them.

In the story of Job, he immediately rebuked his wife in order to nullify her statement inspired by the devil:

> *His wife said to him, "Are you still holding on to your integrity? Curse God and die!" He replied, "You are talking like a foolish woman. Shall we accept good from God, and not trouble?" In all this, Job did not sin in what he said* (Job 2:9-10).

In the case the prophet Micaiah, he also immediately countered the lying spirit that tried to influence him through the mouth of the messenger sent to him:

> *The messenger who had gone to summon Micaiah said to him, "Look, as one man the other prophets are predicting success for the king. Let your word agree with theirs, and speak favorably." But Micaiah said, "As surely as the Lord lives, I can tell him only what the Lord tells me"* (1 Kings 22:13-14).

In both examples, these prophets did not allow the evil decrees to alight on them and so averted their consequences. In simple terms, they refused to cooperate with the evil decrees.

Another way of countering evil decrees is to issue a favorable decree or pronouncement in the same area that the evil decree addresses as in the story of Esther:

At once the royal secretaries were summoned—on the twenty-third day of the third month, the month of Sivan. They wrote out all Mordecai's orders to the Jews, and to the satraps, governors and nobles of the 127 provinces stretching from India to Cush. These orders were written in the script of each province and the language of each people and also to the Jews in their own script and language (Esther 8:9).

The king's edict granted the Jews in every city the right to assemble and protect themselves; to destroy, kill and annihilate any armed force of any nationality or province that might attack them and their women and children; and to plunder the property of their enemies (Esther 8:11).

PERSONAL TESTIMONY

In another dream, an evil person pretending to a messenger of God came to me and said that I needed to put my house in order "because it was time to go home and be with the Lord." I was perplexed because it did not resonate in my spirit. While in the dream I remembered that there were many responsibilities that the Lord has given to me and they were not yet completed. Then the biblical words of the wife of Manoah came to my mind while still in the dream:

And he [Manoah] *said to his wife, "We will certainly die, for we have seen God! But his wife said If the Lord were going to kill us, He would not have accepted our burnt offering and grain offering. He would not have appeared to us and told us this wonderful thing..."* (Judges 13:22-23 NLT).

I said to this person in my dream that I have many assignments from the Lord to carry out on the earth and so why should God want me to return to Heaven before the completion of these assignments. At this, he (the pretend messenger) got angry and suddenly the Lord opened my eyes and I could see he had the legs of a young person even though he pretended to be a wise, old, and frail person. I also noticed that he had jungle boots on. At this point I rebuked him and he immediately disappeared from my presence.

Understanding the Anointing

Anointing is derived from the Hebrew word *Masiah* or *Messiah*, which means "the anointed one." Anointing is the setting apart or consecration for a divine function. It entails the transference of divine power to enable the person to carry out a specified function. It therefore originates from God and is given by His Spirit. In the spirit realm, anointing starts from the verbal proclamation of God concerning such setting apart for the divine function. The Word of God comes as a package that contains within itself the creative and protective ability to bring it to fulfillment.

In the physical realm, anointing is symbolized by the pouring of oil on the head of the one to be anointed or on the object to be consecrated. Applying the oil in the Old Testament is equivalent to baptism in the New Testament, and it is the outward sign that is indicative of an inward grace. In the Old Testament, priests, prophets, and kings were anointed for their calling, but the expression of the anointing was different. The priest was anointed to offer sacrifices and proclaim absolution from sin. The prophet was anointed to speak the words of God, and the king was anointed to rule or govern the people. David was anointed king and *"from that day on, the Spirit of the Lord came upon David in power"* (1 Sam. 16:13). Likewise, sacred objects were set apart and consecrated before they could be used in the service of the house of God.

(For more information see my book *How to Live the Supernatural Life in the Here and Now*.)

DECLARATIONS

"Thou shalt also decree a thing, and it shall be established unto thee..." (Job 22:28 KJV).

1. O God, let the unspoken thought and the spoken words in my mouth be in line with Your will and plans for my life. May they be pleasing and acceptable to You.

   "But how can I ever know what sins are lurking in my heart? Cleanse me from these hidden faults. And keep me from deliberate wrongs, and help me stop doing them. Only then can I be free of guilt and innocent of some great crime. May my spoken words and unspoken thoughts be pleasing even to You, O God my Rock and Redeemer" (Psalm 19:12-14 TLB).

2. God has given me an instructed tongue and my tongue shall bring life to circumstance and death to the evil that may come against me.

   "The Sovereign Lord has given me an instructed tongue, to know the word that sustains the weary. He wakens me morning by morning, wakens my ear to listen like one being taught" (Isaiah 50:4).

   "Reckless words pierce like a sword, but the tongue of the wise brings healing" (Proverbs 12:18).

   "He who guards his mouth and his tongue keeps himself from calamity" (Proverbs 21:23).

   "The tongue has the power of life and death, and those who love it will eat its fruit" (Proverbs 18:21).

   "The tongue that brings healing is a tree of life, but a deceitful tongue crushes the spirit" (Proverbs 15:4).

"David said to the Philistine, 'You come against me with sword and spear and javelin, but I come against you in the name of the Lord Almighty, the God of the armies of Israel, whom you have defied. This day the Lord will hand you over to me, and I'll strike you down and cut off your head. Today I will give the carcasses of the Philistine army to the birds of the air and the beasts of the earth, and the whole world will know that there is a God in Israel'" (1 Samuel 17:45-46).

"May the words of my mouth and the meditation of my heart be pleasing in Your sight, O Lord, my Rock and my Redeemer" (Psalm 19:14).

Chapter 7

PROPHETIC ACTS AND DRAMA—
THE POWER AND DANGER

Recognizing True, False, and Satanic Mimicry

PROPHETIC ACTING AND DRAMA have become very common practices these days. Many have been inspired by the Holy Spirit to carry out these acts without necessarily knowing why. Others have carried out prophetic acting mimicking what they have seen others do! Either way, the truth remains that prophetic acting can carry very significant spiritual powers that need to be properly understood and harnessed as we walk by the Spirit.

A prophetic act is an act, deed, or a mission inspired by the Holy Spirit to bring or facilitate the agenda of Heaven on earth. It carries much more results or implications than would be accomplished by similar but mere physical action. This is because it transcends the realm of the physical and carries strong invisible spiritual implications. Prophetic acting is parallel to establishing spiritual authority in the invisible realm by means of visible physical action with or without pronouncements. By prophetic acting, a mere physical action becomes symbolic of a significant and powerful happening in the spirit realm. Prophetic acts can take different forms ranging from a mere simple action to a more complex drama that is much more difficult to completely comprehend by human beings.

Moses demonstrated the direct bearing of prophetic acting in the physical reality of Israel's military success.

> *The Amalekites came and attacked the Israelites at Rephidim. Moses said to Joshua, "Choose some of our men and go out to fight the Amalekites. Tomorrow I will stand on top of the hill with the staff of God in my hands." So Joshua fought the Amalekites as Moses had ordered, and Moses, Aaron and Hur went to the top of the hill. As long as Moses held up his hands, the Israelites were winning, but whenever he lowered his hands, the Amalekites were winning. When Moses' hands grew tired, they took a stone and put it under him and he sat on it. Aaron and Hur held his hands up—one on one side, one on the other—so that his hands remained steady till sunset. So Joshua overcame the Amalekite army with the sword"* (Exodus 17:8-13).

A prophetic act is an act, deed, or a mission inspired by the Holy Spirit to bring or facilitate the agenda of Heaven on earth.

As Moses' hands stretched heavenward, Joshua's troops prevailed in battle. But after some time his arms grew weary and he dropped them to his side. When he did this, he noticed that the tide of the battle shifted—the Amalekites prevailed. Again Moses stretched his arms toward heaven, bringing the matter before the Lord. Again the battle momentum shifted in favor of Joshua and the Israelites. It became clear to Moses that he must keep his arms stretched toward heaven in prophetic act and prayers if he wanted to open the way for divine intervention in the matter. Moses' symbolic action of raising his staff to the Lord in prophetic mimicry or an act symbolic of victory was connected to and determined Joshua's victory in the physical dimension. In this instance, Moses' prophetic act and prayers on the mountaintop helped to pull down the victory already promised by God and ordained in the heavenlies into the realities of the natural world for the Israelites. Such is the power behind prophetic action or drama.

There are things that are pivotal in the successful accomplishment of any prophetic act. The prophetic act should:

- Be *inspired and guided* by the Holy Spirit.

- Be carried out in faith, because without faith it is impossible to please God.

- Come with *specific instructions for the action to be undertaken,* and the instructions should be strictly adhered to.

The following are three important points about prophetic acting:

1. Prophetic acts can open both the physical and the supernatural realms and also open the person performing the act to the power and authority in the spirit realm whether demonic or godly.

2. Prophetic acts can also mean acting out a word of promise or revelation as though already fulfilled in the physical realm, or the act of applying action to prophecy or word of revelation before its fulfillment.

3. Prophetic acts have roots from ancient times. Paula Price, in her book *The Prophet's Dictionary,* defines Prophetic Drama as *"The delivery of prophesies whereby the prophet acts out the message to underscore either its immediacy or its manifest fulfilment."* And further elaborated on the historical perspectives of prophetic drama: *"Prophetic drama dates back to early human history where the silently transmitted words of the God of the lands of were acted out for their worshippers to conceive what the deity was saying."* [1]

This is what God said in the Book of Hosea: *"I have also spoken to [you by] the prophets, and I have multiplied visions [for you] and [have appealed to you] through* **parables acted out by the prophets** (Hosea 12:10 AMP).

A true prophetic act can be enacted out by human beings or by a celestial being, but it is always under the inspiration of the Spirit of God. In this chapter, I examine what prophetic acts are and how to obtain the justice of God using the prophetic acts or mimicries.

Many spontaneous common physical actions that often carry far-reaching spiritual implications include:

Dancing and Leaping

"Let them praise His name with dancing and make music to Him with tambourine and harp" (Psalm 149:3).

Lifting Hands and Bowing Heads

"Ezra praised the Lord, the great God; and all the people lifted their hands and responded, 'Amen! Amen!' Then they bowed down and worshiped the Lord with their faces to the ground" (Nehemiah 8:6).

Groaning in Prayer

"Not only so, but we ourselves, who have the firstfruits of the Spirit, groan inwardly as we wait eagerly for our adoption as sons, the redemption of our bodies" (Romans 8:23).

"My dear children, for whom I am again in the pains of childbirth until Christ is formed in you" (Galatians 4:19).

Shaking or Trembling

"The jailer called for lights, rushed in and fell trembling before Paul and Silas" (Acts 16:29).

"The sight was so terrifying that Moses said, 'I am trembling with fear'" (Hebrews 12:21).

Intense Weeping

"No one could distinguish the sound of the shouts of joy from the sound of weeping, because the people made so much noise. And the sound was heard far away" (Ezra 3:13).

PROPHETIC ACTS

A prophetic act can be performed during the following conditions:

Intercession

By a prophetic act of sacrificing to the God of the Hebrews, the prophet Samuel interceded for Israel, and the heavens fought on behalf of the Israelites: *"While Samuel was sacrificing the burnt offering, the Philistines drew near to engage Israel in battle. But that day the Lord thundered with loud thunder against the Philistines and threw them into such a panic that they were routed before the Israelites. The men of Israel rushed out of Mizpah and pursued the Philistines, slaughtering them along the way to a point below Beth Car. Then Samuel took a stone and set it up between Mizpah and Shen. He named it Ebenezer, saying, "Thus far has the Lord helped us." So the Philistines were subdued and did not invade Israelite territory again. Throughout Samuel's lifetime, the hand of the Lord was against the Philistines"* (1 Sam. 7:10-13). This is also a prophetic act by blood sacrifice.

Prayers

King Hezekiah's humble act of trusting God in prayers:

Hezekiah received the letter from the messengers and read it. Then he went up to the temple of the Lord and spread it out before the Lord. And Hezekiah prayed to the Lord: "O Lord, God of Israel, enthroned between the cherubim, you alone are God over all the kingdoms of the earth. You have made heaven and earth. Give ear, O Lord, and hear; open your eyes, O Lord, and see; listen to the *words Sennacherib has sent to insult the living God. It is true, O Lord, that the Assyrian kings have laid waste these nations and their lands. They have thrown their gods into the fire and destroyed them, for they were not gods but only wood and stone, fashioned by men's hands. Now, O Lord our God, deliver us from his hand, so that all kingdoms on earth may know that you alone, O Lord, are God." Then Isaiah son of Amoz sent a message to Hezekiah: "This is what the Lord, the God of Israel, says: I have heard your prayer concerning Sennacherib king of Assyria* (2 Kings 19:14-20).*

The Lord heard King Hezekiah's plea:

That night the angel of the Lord went out and put to death a hundred and eighty-five thousand men in the Assyrian camp. When the people got up the next morning—there were all the dead bodies! So Sennacherib king of Assyria broke camp and withdrew. He returned to Nineveh and stayed there. One day, while he was worshiping in the temple of his god Nisroch, his sons Adrammelech and Sharezer cut him down with the sword, and they escaped to the land of Ararat. And Esarhaddon his son succeeded him as king (2 Kings 19:35-37).

Spiritual Warfare

After the defeat of the walled city of Jericho, the Israelites suffered humiliating defeat by the hands of the relatively small city of Ai. When Israel made atonement for their sin, God asked Joshua to performed a prophetic act and they were then able to overtake the city of Ai. God told Joshua to perform a prophetic act in order to facilitate the victory over the City of Ai: *"Then the Lord said to Joshua, "Hold out toward Ai the javelin that is in your hand, for into your hand I will deliver the city." So Joshua held out his javelin toward Ai. As soon as he did this, the men in the ambush rose quickly from their position and rushed forward. They entered the city and captured it and quickly set it on fire"* (Josh. 8:18-19).

For Joshua did not draw back the hand that held out his javelin until he had destroyed all who lived in Ai (Joshua 8:26).

Joshua performed another symbolic action prophetically:

> *Joshua said, "Open the mouth of the cave and bring those five kings out to me." So they brought the five kings out of the cave—the kings of Jerusalem, Hebron, Jarmuth, Lachish and Eglon. When they had brought these kings to Joshua, he summoned all the men of Israel and said to the army commanders who had come with him, "Come here and put your feet on the necks of these kings." So they came forward and placed their feet on their necks. Joshua said to them, "Do not be afraid; do not be discouraged. Be strong and courageous. **This is what the Lord will do to all the enemies you are going to fight.**" Then Joshua struck and killed the kings and hung them on five trees, and they were left hanging on the trees until evening* (Joshua 10:22-26).

Dramatization of Divine Message

The prophet Ahijah launched a dramatic prophetic act signaling God's approval of Jeroboam's rule in Israel. When Jeroboam, then an official at King Solomon's palace, was on his way to Jerusalem, the prophet Ahijah met him and dramatized his message from God to Jeroboam:

> *About that time Jeroboam was going out of Jerusalem, and Ahijah the prophet of Shiloh met him on the way, wearing a new cloak. The two of them were alone out in the country, and Ahijah took hold of the new cloak he was wearing and tore it into twelve pieces. Then he said to Jeroboam, "Take ten pieces for yourself, for this is what the Lord, the God of Israel, says: 'See, I am going to tear the kingdom out of Solomon's hand and give you ten tribes'"* (1 Kings 11:29-31).

This prophetic act was fulfilled later: *"So the king did not listen to the people, for this turn of events was from the Lord, to fulfill the word the Lord had spoken to Jeroboam son of Nebat through Ahijah the Shilonite. When all Israel saw that the king refused to listen to them, they answered the king: "What share do we have in David, what part in Jesse's son? To your tents, O Israel! Look after your own house, O David!" So the Israelites went home"* (1 Kings 12:15-16).

Impartation of Blessing

By prayers and prophetic action, Jacob blessed the sons of Joseph and Ephraim ahead of Manasseh:

Now Israel's eyes were failing because of old age, and he could hardly see. So Joseph brought his sons close to him, and his father kissed them and embraced them. Israel said to Joseph, "I never expected to see your face again, and now God has allowed me to see your children too." Then Joseph removed them from Israel's knees and bowed down with his face to the ground. And Joseph took both of them, Ephraim on his right toward Israel's left hand and Manasseh on his left toward Israel's right hand, and brought them close to him. But Israel reached out his right hand and put it on Ephraim's head, though he was the younger, and crossing his arms, he put his left hand on Manasseh's head, even though Manasseh was the firstborn. Then he blessed Joseph and said, "May the God before whom my fathers Abraham and Isaac walked, the God who has been my Shepherd all my life to this day, the Angel who has delivered me from all harm—may He bless these boys. May they be called by my name and the names of my fathers Abraham and Isaac, and may they increase greatly upon the earth." When Joseph saw his father placing his right hand on Ephraim's head he was displeased; so he took hold of his father's hand to move it from Ephraim's head to Manasseh's head. Joseph said to him, "No, my father, this one is the firstborn; put your right hand on his head." But his father refused and said, "I know, my son, I know. He too will become a people, and he too will become great. Nevertheless, his younger brother will be greater than he, and his descendants will become a group of nations." He blessed them that day and said, "In your name will Israel pronounce this blessing: 'May God make you like Ephraim and Manasseh.'" So he put Ephraim ahead of Manasseh [by prayers] (Genesis 48:10-20).*

Proclamation of a Curse

The prophet Jeremiah used prophetic action to issue a curse on Babylon:

> *Jeremiah had written on a scroll about all the disasters that would come upon Babylon—all that had been recorded concerning Babylon. He said to Seraiah, "When you get to Babylon, see that you read all these words aloud. Then say, 'O Lord, you have said you will destroy this place, so that neither man nor animal will live in it; it will be desolate for ever.' When you finish reading this scroll, tie a stone to it and throw it into the Euphrates. Then say, 'So will Babylon sink to rise no more because of the disaster I will bring upon her. And her people will fall.'" The words of Jeremiah end here* (Jeremiah 51:60-64).

Deliverance from a Curse

The city of Jericho was suffering under the burden of the curse, but the men of the city came to the prophet and he performed a prophetic act and the curse was reversed and the city was delivered from the curse: *"The men of the city said to Elisha, "Look, our lord, this town is well situated, as you can see, but the water is bad and the land is unproductive." "Bring me a new bowl," he said, "and put salt in it." So they brought it to him. Then he went out to the spring and threw the salt into it, saying, "This is what the Lord says: 'I have healed this water. Never again will it cause death or make the land unproductive.'" And the water has remained wholesome to this day, according to the word Elisha had spoken"* (2 Kings 2:19-22).

CARRYING OUT A PROPHETIC ACT

The following conditions are important in carrying out a prophetic act: the need for strict adherence to the instructions and the need for continuous alertness in the spirit.

The conflict between the house of Israel and Aram continued for a very long time. Now Elisha the prophet was on his dying bed; but before his last breath, he performed a prophetic act in intercession on behalf of Israel:

Now Elisha was suffering from the illness from which he died. Jehoash king of Israel went down to see him and wept over him. "My father! My father!" he cried. "The chariots and horsemen of Israel!" Elisha said, "Get a bow and some arrows," and he did so. "Take the bow in your hands," he said to the king of Israel. When he had taken it, Elisha put his hands on the king's hands. "Open the east window," he said, and he opened it. "Shoot!" Elisha said, and he shot. "The Lord's arrow of victory, the arrow of victory over Aram!" Elisha declared. "You will completely destroy the Arameans at Aphek." Then he said, "Take the arrows," and the king took them. Elisha told him, "Strike the ground." He struck it three times and stopped. The man of God was angry with him and said, "You should have struck the ground five or six times; then you would have defeated Aram and completely destroyed it. But now you will defeat it only three times" (2 Kings 13:14-19).

Later this prophecy was fulfilled and led to King Jehoash receiving the justice of God on the issue.

*Hazael king of Aram died, and Ben-Hadad his son succeeded him as king. Then Jehoash son of Jehoahaz recaptured from Ben-Hadad son of Hazael the towns he had taken in battle from his father Jehoahaz. **Three times Jehoash defeated him,** and so he recovered the Israelite towns"* (2 Kings 13:24-25).

In the midst of an anointed presence, ordinary acts can assume prophetic significance. We see this happen in the story of Saul when he tore the garment of the prophet Samuel. The prophet turned round and said it was symbolic of the way the kingdom will torn away from Saul:

As Samuel turned to leave, Saul caught hold of the hem of his robe, and it tore. Samuel said to him, "The Lord has torn the kingdom of Israel from you today and has given it to one of your neighbors—to one better than you (1 Samuel 15:27-28).

What to Avoid During Prophetic Acting

Disobedience or Irreverence to God

The story of Moses and his staff is an example of what to avoid during prophetic acting. *"The Lord said to Moses, 'Take the staff, and you and your brother Aaron gather the assembly together. Speak to that rock before their eyes and it will pour out its water. You will bring water out of the rock for the community so that they and their livestock can drink.' So Moses took the staff from the Lord's presence, just as he commanded him. He and Aaron gathered the assembly together in front of the rock and Moses said to them, 'Listen, you rebels, must we bring you water out of this rock?"* (Num. 20:7-10).

But Moses failed to follow strict instruction: *"Then Moses raised his arm and struck the rock twice with his staff. Water gushed out, and the community and their livestock drank"* (Num. 20:11). For this his punishment was costly, perhaps, to whom much is given much is required.

For this disobedience Moses did not enter the Promised Land: *"But the Lord said to Moses and Aaron, "Because you did not trust in Me enough to honor Me as holy in the sight of the Israelites, you will not bring this community into the land I give them"* (Num. 20:12).

False Prophetic Acting

A false prophetic act is acting out a word or prophecy without the inspiration of the Spirit of God. This can occur in many ways including false prophetic acts that are initiated by the desire to further selfish agendas and with the intention to cause deception.

> *Then the prophet Hananiah took the yoke off the neck of the prophet Jeremiah and broke it, and he said before all the people, "This is what the Lord says: 'In the same way will I break the yoke of Nebuchadnezzar king of Babylon off the neck of all the nations within two years."' At this, the prophet Jeremiah went on his way. Shortly after the prophet Hananiah had broken the yoke off the neck of the prophet Jeremiah,*

the word of the Lord came to Jeremiah: "Go and tell Hananiah, 'This is what the Lord says: You have broken a wooden yoke, but in its place you will get a yoke of iron. This is what the Lord Almighty, the God of Israel, says: I will put an iron yoke on the necks of all these nations to make them serve Nebuchadnezzar king of Babylon, and they will serve him. I will even give him control over the wild animals.'" Then the prophet Jeremiah said to Hananiah the prophet, "Listen, Hananiah! The Lord has not sent you, yet you have persuaded this nation to trust in lies. Therefore, this is what the Lord says: 'I am about to remove you from the face of the earth. This very year you are going to die, because you have preached rebellion against the Lord.'" In the seventh month of that same year, Hananiah the prophet died (Jeremiah 28:10-17).

A false prophetic act is acting out a word or prophecy
without the inspiration of the Spirit of God.

The most common false prophetic acts are usually those based on presumption with no intention to cause deception, but they also attract rebukes from God as God rebuked Job's presumptuous friends: *"After the Lord had said these things to Job, he said to Eliphaz the Temanite, 'I am angry with you and your two friends, because you have not spoken of me what is right...'"* (Job 42:7).

False prophetic acts attract repercussion from God. We must avoid false prophetic acts as they are capable of opening up a person to the intricacies of the power of the dark side of this world—and often lead gradually to demonic entanglement, delusion, and possible harmful effects.

PROPHETIC ACTS BY CELESTIAL BEINGS

Even celestial beings carried out prophetic acts in order to dramatize the overthrow of violence in the notorious city of Babylon: *"Then a mighty angel picked up a boulder the size of a large millstone and threw it into the sea, and said: 'With such violence the great city of Babylon will be thrown down, never to be found again'"* (Rev. 18:21).

RECOGNIZING SATANIC MIMICRY OF PROPHETIC ACTS

Satanic equivalent of prophetic acts, evil enactment, is the satanic counterfeit of prophetic acts and are the actions inspired by the devil or his cohorts. Therefore, these enactments easily open up and establish connection with evil powers in the spirit world. Idol worshiping and demonic incantations are common examples of this practice.

> *He then brought me into the inner court of the house of the Lord, and there at the entrance to the temple, between the portico and the altar, were about twenty-five men. With their backs toward the temple of the Lord and their faces toward the east, they were bowing down to the sun in the east* (Ezekiel 8:16).

Demonic mimicry of prophetic acting: *"When the king of Moab saw that the battle had gone against him, he took with him seven hundred swordsmen to break through to the king of Edom, but they failed. Then he took his firstborn son, who was to succeed him as king, and offered him as a sacrifice on the city wall. The fury against Israel was great; they withdrew and returned to their own land"* (2 Kings 3:26-27).

The descendants of Moab became neighbors of the Israelites and inhabited the eastern border of the Dead Sea. Over the course of history, the Moabites became subjugated to Israel and paid tributes to Israel. When King Mesha rebelled against Israel, the kings of Judah and Edom allied with Israel against Moab. The tide of the battle went seriously against the Moabites. To Mesha, if they were defeated in the battle, it meant only one thing—his god Chemosh was angry with Moab. Consequently, Mesha offered his son, heir to the throne, to his god. The Bible records that the tide of the battle shifted in the direction that King Mesha wanted. Suddenly the Israelites pulled off their attack.

WHAT TO AVOID AS CHRISTIANS

Christians must make conscious efforts to avoid these evil mimicries because whether they are done innocently or not, they are capable of opening up people to tap into the power from the dark side with all its dire consequences. This power can be very alluring as it tends to open up deceptive and instantaneous sources of evil enablement that delude and could lead to crippling bondage.

Christians should avoid any form of enactment that is not inspired by the Holy Spirit. Some such acts may appear to be innocuous; but at the least they are not Christian and could be at times be outright demonic. There are countless ways these unchristian enactments can occur but following are a few of the common forms in which I have seen some Christians involved. These acts have no biblical basis nor are they inspired by the Holy Spirit.

- Writing another person's name on a piece of paper and then burning it, hoping to bring judgment upon that person.
- Writing someone's name on a piece of paper and then writing their own name beside it, hoping to invoke love and bonding.
- Physically standing on a Bible to make a pronouncement, thinking it will carry more power. However, we know that the power of proclamation rests in the right standing of the proclaimer with God and on whether the proclamation lines up with the will of God on the matter.

EVALUATE A PROPHETIC ACT BEFORE CARRYING IT OUT

However, one should not be afraid to carry out an act if prompted by the Holy Spirit. If one is in doubt about having received divine prompting or not, then put the act to the following tests:

- Does it speak of the love of God?
- Does it draw you closer to God?

- Does it enhance the Christ-likeness in you?
- Would Jesus do that?
- Does it stir self-exaltation?
- Does it respect human life, even the life of your enemy?

The power of prophetic acts includes:

- Settling things in the spirit realm before they manifest in the natural realm.
- Quickening the fulfillment of prophecy.
- Putting action to a word or revelation to break the inertia in unfulfilled promises.
- Acting as a thrush momentum to propel spiritual forces.
- Increasing the faith of people.
- Empowering the angelic beings to act on behalf of the saints.

Many prophets of old like Elisha and Zechariah performed some outstanding prophetic acts to facilitate the agenda of Heaven on earth. God directed the prophet Zechariah to perform three specific prophetic mimicries as messages to Israel.

Mimicry	Scripture Reference
Signifying that God is **withdrawing favor or grace** from them	Zechariah 11:7-11 *So I pastured the flock marked for slaughter, particularly the oppressed of the flock. Then I took two staffs and called one **Favor** and the other **Union**, and I pastured the flock. In one month I got rid of the three shepherds. The flock detested me, and I grew weary of them and said, "I will not be your shepherd. Let the dying die, and the perishing perish. Let those who are left eat one another's flesh." Then I took my staff called Favor and broke it, revoking the covenant I had made with all the nations. It was revoked on that day, and so the afflicted of the flock who were watching me knew it was the word of the Lord.*

Mimicry	Scripture Reference
The **bond of unity** between Judah and Israel is **broken**	Zechariah 11:14 *Then I broke my second staff called **Union**, breaking the brotherhood between Judah and Israel.*
Illustrating the role of the **worthless, wicked shepherds** in Israel	**Zechariah 11:15-17** *Then the Lord said to me, "Take again the equipment of a foolish shepherd. For I am going to raise up a shepherd over the land who will not care for the lost, or seek the young, or heal the injured, or feed the healthy, but will eat the meat of the choice sheep, tearing off their hoofs. "Woe to **the worthless shepherd**, who deserts the flock! May the sword strike his arm and his right eye! May his arm be completely withered, his right eye totally blinded!"*

There are many prophetic acts in the Bible. Two examples follow:

A prophetic act by Nehemiah

I and my brothers and my men are also lending the people money and grain. But let the exacting of usury stop! Give back to them immediately their fields, vineyards, olive groves and houses, and also the usury you are charging them—the hundredth part of the money, grain, new wine and oil." "We will give it back," they said. "And we will not demand anything more from them. We will do as you say." Then I summoned the priests and made the nobles and officials take an oath to do what they had promised. **I also shook out the folds of my robe and said, "In this way may God shake out of his house and possessions every man who does not keep this promise. So may such a man be shaken out and emptied!"** *At this the whole assembly said, "Amen," and praised the Lord. And the people did as they had promised* (Nehemiah 5:10-13).

A prophetic act by Agabus

Leaving the next day, we reached Caesarea and stayed at the house of Philip the evangelist, one of the Seven. He had four unmarried daughters who prophesied. After we had been there a number of days, a prophet named Agabus came down from Judea. Coming over to us, he took Paul's belt, tied his own hands and feet with it and said, "The Holy Spirit says, 'In this way the Jews of Jerusalem will bind the owner of this belt and will hand him over to the Gentiles.'" When we heard this, we and the people there pleaded with Paul not to go up to Jerusalem. Then Paul answered, "Why are you weeping and breaking my heart? I am ready not only to be bound, but also to die in Jerusalem for the name of the Lord Jesus." When he would not be dissuaded, we gave up and said, "The Lord's will be done" (Acts 21:8-14).

ENDNOTE

1. Paula Price, *The Prophet's Dictionary* (New Kensington, PA: Whitaker House, 2006), 418.

DECLARATIONS

"Thou shalt also decree a thing, and it shall be established unto thee..."
(Job 22:28 KJV).

1. The Lord is my victory, no matter the strength of the enemy who rises
    up against me; He will help me come out on top every time.

    *"All the nations surrounded me, but in the name of the Lord I cut
    them off. They surrounded me on every side, but in the name of the
    Lord I cut them off. They swarmed around me like bees, but they died
    out as quickly as burning thorns; in the name of the Lord I cut them
    off"* (Psalm 118:10-12).

    *"The Lord will make you the head, not the tail. If you pay attention to
    the commands of the Lord your God that I give you this day and care-
    fully follow them, you will always be at the top, never at the bottom"*
    (Deuteronomy 28:13).

    *"For the Lord God is a sun and shield; the Lord bestows favor and
    honor; no good thing does he withhold from those whose walk is
    blameless"* (Psalm 84:11).

2. God will meet all my needs according His riches in glory by Christ Jesus
    and He will watch over me to perform His words concerning me.

    *"And my God will meet all your needs according to His glorious riches
    in Christ Jesus"* (Philippians 4:19).

    *"The Lord said to me, 'You have seen correctly, for I am watching to
    see that My word is fulfilled'"* (Jeremiah 1:12).

Part II

The
Heavenly
Courts
of
God
and
Accessing
Blessings

Chapter 8

THE HEAVENLY
COURTS OF GOD

Picture what it would look like if you were to suddenly find yourself in a court-like audience with God. Many people have had these court-like sessions with God in their dreams or visions. The Bible is also full of instances of these occurrences. Bible instances of people who have had experiences of spiritual court scenarios in their dreams or visions are many. Some writers have said these experiences constitute a *heavenly court system*.

One of the most notable of these encounters is in the Book of Daniel. The prophet Daniel described a swift assembly of a court of God in the heavenly realm in response to the boastful horn that he saw in his dream:

> *While I was thinking about the horns, there before me was another horn, a little one, which came up among them; and three of the first horns were uprooted before it. This horn had eyes like the eyes of a man and a mouth that spoke boastfully. As I looked, thrones were set in place, and the Ancient of Days took his seat. His clothing was as white as snow; the hair of his head was white like wool. His throne*

was flaming with fire, and its wheels were all ablaze. A river of fire was flowing, coming out from before him. Thousands upon thousands attended him; ten thousand times ten thousand stood before him. The court was seated, and the books were opened. Then I continued to watch because of the boastful words the horn was speaking. I kept looking until the beast was slain and its body destroyed and thrown into the blazing fire. (The other beasts had been stripped of their authority, but were allowed to live for a period of time.) In my vision at night I looked, and there before me was one like a son of man, coming with the clouds of heaven. He approached the Ancient of Days and was led into His presence. He was given authority, glory and sovereign power; all peoples, nations and men of every language worshiped Him. His dominion is an everlasting dominion that will not pass away, and His kingdom is one that will never be destroyed (Daniel 7:8-14).

The prophet Daniel also saw how the justice of God would follow such a court-like audience with God: *"until the Ancient of Days came and pronounced judgment in favor of the saints of the Most High, and the time came when they possessed the kingdom"* (Daniel 7:22).

But the court will sit, and his power will be taken away and completely destroyed forever. Then the sovereignty, power and greatness of the kingdoms under the whole heaven will be handed over to the saints, the people of the Most High. His kingdom will be an everlasting kingdom, and all rulers will worship and obey Him (Daniel 7:26-27).

It appears that these court-like audiences with God are not haphazard but rather more like a concerted divine approach to intervene in a way that ensures supreme justice in this wicked world. Because it is divinely orchestrated, one cannot predict its initiation, occurrence, or any particular regularity, but it always originates from God. In a sense, it is a beacon of hope in this evil world. The Psalmist says God's throne is *"forever and ever. A sceptre of righteousness is the sceptre of His kingdom. He love righteousness and hate wickedness"* (Ps. 45:6-7 NKJV).

If we can call these court-like audiences with God a system, then this system is a supreme judicial one that is incorruptible because it is always initiated and headed by the omniscient, omnipotent, and omnipresent God. The supremacy of God is anchored on the justice of God and His desire to be seen as just; as the prophet Isaiah said, "...*For the Lord is a God of justice...*" (Isa. 30:18). These court-like scenes are about the supreme justice of God in action. In the Scriptures we see a picture of God who is not only supreme but is just and always seeks to make manifest His justice to everyone. This is the core of the manifold wisdom of God, namely His righteousness, justice, and supremacy centered on divine fairness. It appears that in line with this, these audiences are spiritual court scenarios in which God presides.

Though the term *heavenly court* is not used in the Bible, there are other names in the Scriptures that describe this system. *For instance,* the *counsel of the Lord* is mentioned in the Book of Jeremiah: *"For who hath stood in the **counsel of the Lord**, and hath perceived and heard his word? Who hath marked His word, and heard it?"* (Jer. 23:18 KJV). And *"But if they had stood in **My counsel** and had caused My people to hear My words, then they should have turned them from their evil way and from the evil of their doings"* (Jer. 23:22 KJV). *The council of God* is revealed in Psalm 89:7: *"In the **council of** the holy ones **God** is greatly feared; He is more awesome than all who surround Him".*

However, direct references to court in the *spiritual realm* are found in several instances in the Bible: *"I kept looking until thrones were placed [for the assessors with Judge], and the Ancient of Days, [God, the eternal Father] took His seat, whose garment was white as snow and the hair of his head like pure wool. His throne was like the fiery flame; its wheels were burning fire. A stream of fire came forth from before Him, a thousand thousands ministered to Him and ten thousand times ten thousand rose up and stood before Him; the Judge was seated, [**the court was in session**] and the books were opened"* (Dan. 7:9-10 AMP).

Also in Zechariah 3:7: *"This is what the Lord Almighty says: 'If you will walk in my ways and keep my requirements, then you will **govern my house and have charge of my courts**, and I will give you a place among these standing here."*

In several other instances, even though the word *court* was not used, the pattern, operations, and subsequent pronouncements emanating from some spiritual sessions or encounters bear credence to the existence of court-like scenes in heavenly places.

It is important to note that these court-like audiences entail spiritual court sessions in which God presides as the Judge. Perhaps apostle James alluded to this when he said; "*There is only one Lawgiver and Judge, the One who is able save and destroy*" (James 4:12a). Therefore, judgments from these courts are fair and are balanced perspectives of the situations and events because they emanate from God's presence and judgment. In these heavenly courts everything is laid bare, as God is the Judge. Even satan intrigues; craftiness and schemes are exposed and disappointed in these courts: "*Nothing in all creation is hidden from God's sight. Everything is uncovered and laid bare before the eyes of Him to whom we must give account*" (Heb. 4:13).

This heavenly court system is all-powerful in accordance with the nature of the Judge of the universe who will one day enforce His justice in this world. This court system stands above and towers over the corruptive and manipulative schemes of satan and this perishing world. Biblical examples abound and together with the countless real-life experiences of this system, we see glimpses of a truly divine court system that offers us clues as to how a perfect justice can actually operate in an imperfect earth. I have experienced a few of what I describe as heavenly courts encounters. One of these encounters happened at a time in my life when I was at a crossroad and in desperate need of divine intervention to decide whether to go right or left. At that time I was offered a job in city that I did not think would enhance my spiritual life, yet the job was exactly what I needed at the time.

In dreamlike state I found myself in what I recall as the presence of God. I don't know how I could tell this but somehow my spirit said it was His presence. Then He said to me to take the job and relocate to the city. But He also said to me to put Isaiah 54 into a song. I replied how He knows that I am not a good singer, but if He permits me, I would put at least one of the verses into a song. He insisted that His instruction was for me to put the whole chapter into a song. That was the end of our court-like session. While still in the dream, I felt intrigued by this and was eager to get home to tell my wife what the Lord had just told me. On the way home I noticed a congregation in worship. I decided to join them and when I was in their midst I discovered that they were singing Isaiah 54 and were in verse two: "Enlarge the place of your tent." Then I woke up. We obeyed the Lord's instruction and relocated to the city. Curiously, the sermon being delivered in the first church I visited in that city was on Isaiah 54.

As in any court system, in this spiritual court system both the wicked and the righteous can be present, but **one thing is constant—the judge of every heavenly court is God,** as the Bible says, *"...You have come to **God, the Judge of all men,** to the spirits of the righteous men made perfect"* (Heb. 12:23b). And *"The Lord has established His throne in heaven and **His kingdom rules over all"*** (Ps. 103:19). *"God presides in the great assembly; He gives **judgment among the gods"*** (Ps. 82:1).

The pillar of this awesome system, and that which makes it more powerful than any evil power, is that the only one qualified to be the presiding Judge is God. This divine system stands above and towers over the corruptive and manipulative schemes of satan and the system of this world. Bible examples give us glimpses of the existence of this heavenly court system that is incorruptible and also offers us the chance to see how the system actually operates on earth.

We see where the court was assembled in a swift response to the actions of men on earth that requires immediate attention and judgment from God (see Dan. 7:8-14), and at other times, there is insinuation that some heavenly courts are perhaps held on a regular basis (see Zech. 3:7). As for the composition of these courts, some have large numbers of participants and others seem to have as few as only two participants. The composition is highly variable and the participants could be of varied background.

> *Far be it from you to do such a thing—to kill the righteous with the wicked, treating the righteous and the wicked alike. Far be it from you! Will not the Judge of all the earth do right?* (Genesis 18:25)

There is a further allusion that affirms the supremacy of God in the Book of Colossians: *"For by him all things were created: things in heaven and on earth, visible and invisible, whether thrones or powers or rulers or authorities; all things were created by Him and for Him. **He is before all things, and in Him all things hold together"*** (Col. 1:16-17).

In some cases, those under the judgment of God may participate directly, but in other cases they are represented via prophetic representation or intercession. This is in accordance with the principle of prophetic privilege of intercession. It is possible that these spiritual court sessions can be held in the third heaven and outside the third heaven as in the heavenly places. Apostle Paul had a vision of the Throne Room of Judgment in Revelation 20:4:

> *I saw thrones on which were seated those who had been given authority to judge. And I saw the souls of those who had been beheaded because of their testimony for Jesus and because of the word of God. They had not worshiped the beast or his image and had not received his mark on their foreheads or their hands. They came to life and reigned with Christ a thousand years.*

The Throne Room's Heavenly Courts

And the prophet Micaiah saw a court session in the Throne Room in First Kings 22:19-22.

> *Micaiah continued, "Therefore hear the word of the Lord: I saw the Lord sitting on His throne with all the host of heaven standing around Him on His right and on His left. And the Lord said, 'Who will entice Ahab into attacking Ramoth Gilead and going to his death there?' One suggested this, and another that. Finally, a spirit came forward, stood before the Lord and said, 'I will entice him.' 'By what means?' the Lord asked. 'I will go out and be a lying spirit in the mouths of all his prophets,' he said. 'You will succeed in enticing him,' said the Lord. Go and do it."*

In heavenly courts everything is laid bare before God, nothing is hidden; even satan's lies at these courts are exposed. The verdicts that come from these courts *cannot be contravened*, even the devil is compelled to comply with them. This is illustrated in the story of Job; at first satan was given the permission during a heavenly court session only to penetrate the divine hedge that surrounded Job and touch his possessions but not his body. *"But stretch out your hand and strike everything he has, and he will surely curse You to Your face,"* satan said. The Lord said to satan, *"Very well, then, everything he has is in your hands, but on the man himself do not lay a finger."* *Then satan went out from the presence of the Lord* (Job 1:11-12).

Later satan appeared in another heavenly court and was given extended permission to touch Job's body, but God forbade him to take his life: *"Skin for skin!" Satan replied. "A man will give all he has for his own life. But stretch out Your hand and strike his flesh and bones, and he will surely curse You to your face." The Lord said to Satan, "Very well, then, he is in your hands; but you must spare his life"* (Job 2:4-6).

In heavenly courts everything is laid bare before God, nothing is hidden; even satan's lies at these courts are exposed.

PRIEST JOSHUA VINDICATED, SATAN REBUKED

In the Book of Zechariah, the prophet Zechariah saw a heavenly courtroom in action where Joshua, representing the people of Judah, was standing before the Angel of the Lord and was being accused by satan:

> *Then he showed me Joshua the high priest standing before the angel of the Lord, and Satan standing at his right side to accuse him. The Lord said to Satan, "The Lord rebuke you, Satan! The Lord, who has chosen Jerusalem, rebuke you! Is not this man a burning stick snatched from the fire?" Now Joshua was dressed in filthy clothes as he stood before the angel. The angel said to those who were standing before him, "Take off his filthy clothes." Then he said to Joshua, "See, I have taken away your sin, and I will put rich garments on you." Then I said, "Put a clean turban on his head." So they put a clean turban on his head and clothed him, while the angel of the Lord stood by. The angel of the Lord gave this charge to Joshua: "This is what the Lord Almighty says: 'If you will walk in my ways and keep my requirements, then you will govern my house and have charge of my courts,*

and I will give you a place among these standing here (Zechariah 3:1-7).

The cleansing of Joshua was not complete with the removal of his dirty clothes or sin soiled garments, but completion came only when God replaced the dirty clothes with clean garments. This is a symbolic representation of the removal of sin by the atoning blood of Jesus Christ, and His righteousness is imputed to us.

The heavenly court system does not only deal with issues at governmental levels but it extends beyond into personal issues. In fact, most of the interactive dreams and visions that are recorded in Scripture and in some real-life experiences of many people are heavenly courts sessions, though most of these people may not realize the depth of the significance of these revelations. *An interactive dream or vision is one in which God shows up and the dreamer is able to interact and exchange views with God during the encounter (court-like interactive encounter with God).*

The verdicts that come from these courts cannot be *contravened,* even the devil is compelled to comply with them.

PARTICIPANTS AND EDICTS FROM THE COURTS OF GOD

God is the only constant participant in these heavenly court sessions, others are variables. Biblical examples of those who participated in these courts include the prophets, whether they were alive at the time of the encounter or not. For instance, the prophets Zechariah, Habakkuk, Moses, and Micaiah participated or had these court-like experiences during their lifetime. Other non-prophetic people were divinely determined as in the case of King Abimelech. Angelic beings include the common angels, the cherubim and the seraphim. And the cloud of witnesses including the apostles, prophets, and the saints who are in Heaven.

The angel of the Lord gave this charge to Joshua: "This is what the Lord Almighty says: 'If you will walk in my ways and keep my requirements, then you will govern my house and have charge of my courts, and I will give you a place among these standing here (Zechariah 3:6-7).

The twelve disciples of Jesus Christ were also participants as in apostle John receiving the Book of Revelation: *"When I saw Him, I fell at His feet as though dead. Then He placed His right hand on me and said: "Do not be afraid. I am the First and the Last. I am the Living One; I was dead, and behold I am alive for ever and ever! And I hold the keys of death and Hades. "Write, therefore, what you have seen, what is now and what will take place later"* (Rev. 1:17-19).

Also the twenty-four elders: *"Surrounding the throne were twenty-four other thrones, and seated on them were twenty-four elders. They were dressed in white and had crowns of gold on their heads* (Rev. 4:4). Who are these twenty-four elders? They are probably made up of the patriarchs of the twelve tribes of Israel in the Old Testament and the twelve apostles in the New Testament. The significance of this is that twenty-four elders would indicate the redeemed Church of all times, whether before or after the death of Christ.

The devil also participates: *"One day the angels came to present themselves before the Lord, and Satan also came with them. The Lord said to Satan, 'Where have you come from?' Satan answered the Lord, 'From roaming through the earth and going to and fro in it.' Then the Lord said to Satan, 'Have you considered my servant Job? There is no one on earth like him; he is blameless and upright, a man who fears God and shuns evil' "* (Job 1:6-8).

And evil spirits: *"'By what means?' the Lord asked. 'I will go out and be a lying spirit in the mouths of all his prophets,' he said. 'You will succeed in enticing him,' said the Lord. 'Go and do it'"* (1 Kings 22:22).

The heavenly court system does not only deal with issues at governmental levels but it extends beyond into personal issues.

SPIRITUAL NON-COURT CONGREGATIONS

In the heavenly realm, there are other assemblies in which God is not the presiding judge. I call these spiritual non-court congregations or gatherings. Nevertheless, their sessions and their resultant decrees affect and determine the course of events in the tangible and visible world of the earth. Decrees from these congregations generally reflect the interest of the participants and are always slanted toward the objectives of the group. Therefore the edicts from them are biased and lack fairness.

God is the only constant participant in heavenly
court sessions, others are variables.

CONGREGATION OF THE RIGHTEOUS

The Bible speaks of these assemblies of the righteous in many instances in the Scriptures, so let us look at a few examples:

Assembly of the Righteous

Therefore the wicked will not stand in the judgment, nor sinners in the assembly of the righteous (Psalm 1:5).

Company of Angels

The Bible says that Jacob suddenly ran into a company of angels and he was astonished at the awesome sight:

Jacob also went on his way, and the angels of God met him. When Jacob saw them, he said, "This is the camp of God!" So he named that place Mahanaim (Genesis 32:1-2).

Transfiguration of Jesus Christ

Jesus, during His transfiguration, was in the company of Moses and Elijah. This happened in His capacity as the Son of Man and they encouraged Him for the fate He was about to face. Later the voice of God was interjected into the visionary encounter.

> *About eight days after Jesus said this, He took Peter, John and James with Him and went up onto a mountain to pray. As He was praying, the appearance of His face changed, and His clothes became as bright as a flash of lightning. Two men, Moses and Elijah, appeared in glorious splendour, talking with Jesus. They spoke about His departure, which He was about to bring to fulfillment at Jerusalem* (Luke 9:28-31).

Council of the Wicked. The Bible also records assemblies of the wicked or evil ones. Examples follow.

Congregation of the Sinners

> *Blessed is the man who does not walk in the counsel of the wicked or stand in the way of sinners or sit in the seat of mockers* (Psalm 1:1).

Council of the Violent People

> *Simeon and Levi are brothers—their swords are weapons of violence. Let me not enter their council, let me not join their assembly, for they have killed men in their anger and hamstrung oxen as they pleased* (Genesis 49:5-6).

EDICT CHARACTERISTICS

There are edicts from the heavenly places that are continually being released. However, the verdicts from the heavenly court system (spiritual court over which

God presides) have a more balanced perspective of things because they always contain God's viewpoint. They are very powerful and will never return void to God. We are required to respond appropriately to them. They are not usually irrevocable, for we can appeal to God over the issues revealed. On a few occasions, the edicts from heavenly courts may be outright irrevocable that we cannot change.

Edicts from the heavenly court system could be characterized as follows:

- Edicts are powerful, approved, and sanctioned by God.
- Edicts are not generally irrevocable.
- Appealing to God can alter edicts.
- We respond or cooperate with edicts in the natural realm.
- Edicts do not return to God void.
- Some edicts are irrevocable, only requiring compliance.
- Edicts cannot be contravened.

God's edicts are issued to pluck up and overthrow things contrary to His Kingdom. Like His commandments, God's decrees can also be dispensed to build and plant according to Kingdom plans and principles. Spiritual confrontation in the heavenly places is actually the struggle of uprooting and overthrowing evil planting and building and establishing God's decrees in the spirit realm.

EDICTS FROM SPIRITUAL NON-COURT SYSTEMS

These edicts are spiritual court scenes in the heavenly places in which God did not preside. These edicts can be equally powerful however, because of the partiality inherent in their composition and group interest; they are by nature usually unfair and biased. Some of these edicts are evil because they don't emanate from balanced perspectives. However, they can carry profound consequences in our natural world. These decrees are spiritual arrows of variable powers. We must resist the evil edicts with our shield of faith, which is capable of quenching the fiery darts of the enemy. The following are three useful examples.

Good edict from an evil king:

Therefore I decree that the people of any nation or language who say anything against the God of Shadrach, Meshach and Abednego be cut into pieces and their houses be turned into piles of rubble, for no other god can save in this way (Daniel 3:29).

Evil edict from the wickedness of men:

So the administrators and the satraps went as a group to the king and said: "O King Darius, live for ever! The royal administrators, prefects, satraps, advisers and governors have all agreed that the king should issue an edict and enforce the decree that anyone who prays to any god or man during the next thirty days, except to you, O king, shall be thrown into the lions' den (Daniel 6:6-7).

Another good edict from an evil king:

I issue a decree that in every part of my kingdom people must fear and reverence the God of Daniel. "For He is the living God and He endures for ever; His kingdom will not be destroyed, His dominion will never end (Daniel 6:26).

GOD'S SWIFT JUSTICE BY HEAVENLY COURT SYSTEMS IN THE LAST DAYS

The central purpose of God's emerging swift justice is the preservation of the righteous and to avoid abomination that could cause desolation. Rightly so as the apostle Paul says, *"For the Lord will carry out His sentence on earth with speed and finality. It is just as Isaiah said previously; unless the Lord Almighty had left us descendants, we would have become like Sodom; we would have been like Gomorrah"* (Rom. 9:28-29). Thank God He did not leave us alone.

In the Scriptures we see many instances that bear credence to the fact that if God had not swiftly intervened, abomination of great proportion would have occurred! Evil is escalating in these last days and the need for swift, divine intervention has increased exponentially; where sin abounds, grace abounds much more also (see Rom. 5:20b).

In an instance of the swift justice of God, King Abimelech was acquitted as innocent in the court of God. The story of Abraham's dubious wisdom of lying about the status of his wife, Sarah, and subsequent action of an innocent King Abimelech who unknowingly wanted to take Sarah as his wife, illustrates this system in operation. God resolved this delicate issue and maintained supreme justice by stepping into a heavenly court session that came to King Abimelech in the form of an interactive dream.

> *Now Abraham moved on from there into the region of the Negev and lived between Kadesh and Shur. For a while he stayed in Gerar, and there Abraham said of his wife Sarah, "She is my sister." Then Abimelech king of Gerar sent for Sarah and took her. But God came to Abimelech in a dream one night and said to him, "You are as good as dead because of the woman you have taken; she is a married woman." Now Abimelech had not gone near her, so he said, "Lord, will you destroy an innocent nation? Did he not say to me, 'She is my sister,' and didn't she also say, 'He is my brother'? I have done this with a clear conscience and clean hands." Then God said to him in the dream, "Yes, I know you did this with a clear conscience, and so I have kept you from sinning against me. That is why I did not let you touch her. Now return the man's wife, for he is a prophet, and he will pray for you and you will live. But if you do not return her, you may be sure that you and all yours will die" (Genesis 20:1-7).*

You can imagine what would have happened if King Abimelech had disregarded the verdict from this night encounter with God.

In another instance intervention, the young Solomon quickly became endowed with incredible wisdom from his God encounter. The story of Solomon's interactive dream one night in the court of God is recorded in the first Book of Kings chapter 3.

Israel's golden age as a nation came under the rulership of King Solomon and this period is often remembered with nostalgia by the Israelites. The pleasantry of the golden period is largely embellished by the divine wisdom Solomon received. This is how Solomon became imparted with rare high-level divine wisdom in the court of God that came to him as a dream: *"The king went to Gibeon to offer sacrifices, for that was the most important high place, and Solomon offered a thousand burnt offerings on that altar. **At Gibeon the Lord appeared to Solomon during the night in a dream**, and God said, 'Ask for whatever you want Me to give you'"* (1 Kings 3:4-5).

Solomon's reply has become a classic statement of wisdom, humility, and dependence on God:

> *Solomon answered, "You have shown great kindness to your servant, my father David, because he was faithful to You and righteous and upright in heart. You have continued this great kindness to him and have given him a son to sit on his throne this very day. Now, O Lord my God, You have made Your servant king in place of my father David. But I am only a little child and do not know how to carry out my duties. Your servant is here among the people You have chosen, a great people, too numerous to count or number. So give Your servant a discerning heart to govern Your people and to distinguish between right and wrong. For who is able to govern this great people of Yours?"* (1 Kings 3:6-9)

The Lord was pleased that Solomon had asked for this. So God said to him, *"Since you have asked for this and not for long life or wealth for yourself, nor have asked for the death of your enemies but for discernment in administering justice"* (1 Kings 3:10-11).

The manifestation of the impartation from this encounter was immediate, and the people were also swift to acknowledge the supernatural wisdom that came upon him from this point. *"When all Israel heard the verdict the king had given, they held the king in awe, because they saw that he had wisdom from God to administer justice"* (1 Kings 3:28).

So what began as Solomon's one-night encounter in the court of God later transcended into a national phenomenon and ultimately into a timeless classic in the expression of divine wisdom on the earth. Though the story of Solomon has this pleasant beginning, it took a dramatic downturn. He slid into error through excesses and over-indulgence.

Another example of God's swift justice was when Laban was apprehended to a session in the court of God when Laban was in pursuit of Jacob. Rightly so, it was unfair to Laban that Jacob left his place without his knowledge. Laban should not have been denied the privilege of saying farewell to his daughters. But see how beautifully the supreme and just God handled the matter. Remember, Jacob is the carrier of Abraham's blessing, *"through which all the families of the earth will be blessed"* and therefore God would not allow a curse on such a person so that the blessing may not contaminated.

I believe that Jacob was wrong on this issue of leaving Laban's place. On the other hand, Laban has previously been less than honest with Jacob on many counts. But God settled all these in a heavenly court hearing:

> *Laban didn't learn of their flight for three days. Then, taking several men with him, he set out in hot pursuit and caught up with them seven days later, at Mount Gilead. That night God appeared in a dream "Watch out what you say to Jacob," he was told. "Don't give him your blessing and don't curse him"* (Genesis 31:22-24 TLB).

Notice the outworking of divine justice in this case. As a result of Jacob's error, Laban (his father-in-law) was instructed not to bless him, but Laban was also forbidden to curse him perhaps because he is the carrier of Abraham's covenant.

DECLARATIONS

"Thou shalt also decree a thing, and it shall be established unto thee..." (Job 22:28 KJV).

1. I have hope that He who promised is able to fulfill what He has promised concerning me. My hope will never fail me for my hope is in God.

   "...there may yet be hope" (Lamentations 3:29).

2. The Lord will grant me victory over every courtroom lie.

   "You will have justice against every courtroom lie" (Isaiah 54:17 TLB).

   "The wicked lie in wait for the righteous seeking their very lives; but the Lord will not leave them in their power or let them be condemned when brought to trial" (Psalm 37:32-33).

Chapter 9

Accessing Your Blessings

SATAN IS ALWAYS POISED to deny us of our blessings, and receiving them is often the bone of contention and underlies most of the confrontations in the spiritual realm. The Bible says we were wonderfully and fearfully made. God is eager for us to have life abundantly and flourish in our divine blessings, but the devil wants to deny us of these divine blessings and plunder our inheritance on earth. He wants to destroy the dominion that God has given to man on the earth. Consequently, when we pull divine blessings from the spirit realm into the realities of our lives, we tilt the balance toward the plans and purposes of God, bringing the justice of God into the realities of our lives.

Fulfillment of any divine promise belongs to God. But it is man's responsibility to work that process toward its fulfillment. If we work the process, we hasten the fulfillment, and if we renege on the process, we delay or hinder or even cancel the promise.

There were times in my life, when I noticed that most of the warning revelations were not being averted and the revelations about blessings were not being fulfilled. I sought the face of God over these issues. I was pleasantly surprised with the simple answer He gave to me. God revealed to me that I lived in fear of the warning revelations rather than taking dominion over them by faith. And for the blessings that were not fulfilled, I was quick to celebrate them, while also quick to forget about them as though they had already happened without proper prayer backup. This revelation changed my life as I came to realize the truth that when a blessing is divinely released it becomes available in the spiritual realm without necessarily manifesting in the physical realm.

Fulfillment of any divine promise belongs to God.

That is why the Bible says we have spiritual blessings in heavenly places (see Eph. 1:3). It is our responsibility to correctly appropriate our blessings and pull them down to the realities of our lives by fervent and effective prayers. Revelations will often show to us the blessings that exist in the heavenly realm and so prompts us to their availability in the heavenly realm. Blessings are important, more valuable than money, stronger than any earthly power, and surpass any manner of learning; we should work them into our lives. Blessing is the empowerment to achieve success, a divine enabling to achieve success

Understanding the Nature of Blessing

A blessing or a curse has duality of existence. Both can exist in the spirit without manifestation in the physical realm. This characteristic makes blessings and curses have operational duality. On one hand, they can exist only in the heavenly places without physical manifestation but are also capable manifesting in both realms. When they exist in both realms, they are said to have full expression. Blessings need to be appropriated, and curses without a cause cannot alight on its intended victim. Because of this duality, blessings or curses can skip a generation without manifestation if the required conditions for its expression in the natural realm are not met even though it continues to exist in the spirit realm. Consequently, there are many blessings in the heavenly places that are yet to be pulled down to manifestation in the natural realm, and there are curses that should not be allowed to alight on us.

Soberly, also because of this duality of existence, we must realize that a blessing can be cursed in a way that affects its outworking in the natural manifestations even though it continues to exist in the spirit realm.

> *"If you do not listen, and if you do not set your heart to honor My name," says the Lord Almighty, "I will send a curse upon you, and I will curse your blessings. Yes, I have already cursed them, because you have not set your heart to honor Me* (Malachi 2:2).

The Bible makes the difference in the dynamics of curses and blesses superbly clear when it says, *"those the Lord blesses will inherit the land, but those He curses will be cut off"* (Ps. 37:22).

It is our responsibility to correctly appropriate our blessings and pull them down to the realities of our lives by fervent and effective prayers.

RECEIVE, OR PULL DOWN, YOUR BLESSINGS

A blessing can be held up in the heavenly realm as we see in Daniel:

> *Then he continued, "Do not be afraid, Daniel. Since the first day that you set your mind to gain understanding and to humble yourself before your God, your words were heard, and I have come in response to them. But the prince of the Persian kingdom resisted me twenty-one days. Then Michael, one of the chief princes, came to help me, because I was detained there with the king of Persia. Now I have come to explain to you what will happen to your people in the future, for the vision concerns a time yet to come"* (Daniel 10:12-14).

The continuous prayers of Daniel enabled the angels to overcome the evil principality of Persia that held up the answer to his prayers. By prayers we can connect with the heavenly to pull down our blessing.

The first thing to do in preparing to receive our blessings is to ensure that every negative stronghold in our lives is eliminated. Negative strongholds are the landing pads for curses and are major hindrances to the pulling down of our blessings. Negative strongholds include fears, bitterness, jealousy, unforgiveness, anger, or covetousness. *"The weapons we fight with are not the weapons of the world. On the contrary, they have divine power to demolish strongholds"* (2 Cor. 10:4).

Likewise, obedience to God, a willing heart and a life surrendered to Jesus Christ are the landing pads of blessings in our lives. *"Come now, let us reason together,"* says the Lord. *"Though your sins are like scarlet, they shall be as white as snow; though they are red as crimson, they shall be like wool.* ***If you are willing and obedient, you will eat the best from the land*** (Isa. 1:18-19).

A blessing or a curse has duality of existence. Both can exist in the spirit without manifestation in the physical realm.

The Scripture is replete with instances where the things we do in the natural impinges on the things that transpire in the spirit realm and vice versa, because a constant connection between the physical and the spiritual worlds exists. And only those who know and are conversant with this connection can channel it for the advancement of the purposes of God on earth. Moses in his days utilized it against the Amelekites:

> *Moses said to Joshua, "Choose some of our men and go out to fight the Amalekites. Tomorrow I will stand on top of the hill with the staff of God in my hands." So Joshua fought the Amalekites as Moses had ordered, and Moses, Aaron and Hur went to the top of the hill. As long as Moses held up his hands, the Israelites were winning, but*

whenever he lowered his hands, the Amalekites were winning (Exodus 17:9-11).

Moses demonstrated in this process that there is direct connection between the supernatural and the things that happen in the natural realm.

How to Appropriate Adamic Blessing

Adamic blessing precedes the much talked about blessing of Abraham. Adamic blessing is the blessing that commonly accrues from or is often associated with the degree of innocence or spiritual purity of a person and whether or not the person lives a life of continuous repentance. The blessing of Adam was also the first prophetic blessing given by God to man. In it, God spoke of subduing and taking dominion when everything was yet in the unpolluted state of righteousness, peace, joy, and heightened level of spirituality. This was the atmosphere that prevailed in the Garden of Eden immediately following the creation of man. It was prophetic because by inference, God gave enablement to man to bring into order any insurrection or disorder that may arise on earth. Any tendency for anything or event to go into defiance of the will of God can be subdued using the principles and power inherent in this blessing. This blessing was so powerful that satan in his jealousy sought to stop man from continuing to enjoy it.

> *Be fruitful, multiply, and fill the earth, and subdue it, using all its vast resources in the service of God and man; and have dominion over the fish of the sea, the birds of the air, and over every living creature that moves upon the earth* (Genesis 1:28 AMP).

I have often found this Bible verse in Genesis to be of great help whenever I needed to counter the evil of a danger that has been revealed to me. It is a prophetic blessing of special empowerment by which, if well appropriated, the redeemed man can regain the dominion that Adam lost to satan and prevail even in difficult circumstances. The key points of this blessing are in its availability to Christians through redemption by the blood of Jesus Christ. We can again subdue and take dominion over any insurrection of the enemy, which could manifest as impending or present danger in our lives as we walk with God. It is therefore a valuable asset as a Bible verse to proclaim when warring over revealed danger or warning revelations. At least, this has been my story.

ACTIVATION OF PROMISES OR BLESSINGS

Activation of promises in our lives could be by verbal proclamation at the very least or by performing prophetic act or mimicry as inspired by the Holy Spirit in relation to its eventual fulfillment. On this point, always remember to wait for the prompting of the Holy Spirit and usually the prompting would come as rhema. The first thing in the process of activation is to give voice to the promises of God in our lives by declaring them to the hearing witnesses in the natural realm. In practical terms, activation of promises usually begins with verbal declaration of the inspired words.

As mentioned in a previous chapter, prophetic acts involve the acting out of the revealed words or prophecies in the natural realm. It is like appointing action to the inspired word or promises in the physical world.

The process of activation involves:

- Simple things of our thought process or the power of holy imagination of seeing the promises of God by the eye of faith while yet in the invisible realm.
- Embracing the promise and meditating or pondering on it.
- Confessing, because through our prophetic confession or proclamation on earth, the angels are enabled to battle the forces of darkness, particularly when the confession lines up with the will of God.

This process of activation can thwart or hinder the evil plans by accelerating the birthing of promises.

The Scripture is full of examples of what other people did in order to pull down their blessings. Here are some we should emulate.

We should have Abraham's kind of faith. *"Against all hope, Abraham in hope believed and so became the father of many nations, just as it had been said to him, 'So shall your offspring be.' Without weakening in his faith, he faced the fact that his body* *was as good as dead—since he was about a hundred years old—and that Sarah's womb was also dead. Yet he did not waver through unbelief regarding the promise of God, but was strengthened in his faith and gave glory to God, being fully persuaded that God had power to do what He had promised. This is why 'it was credited to him as righteousness'"* (Rom. 4:18-22).

We should have Moses' kind of commitment. *"By faith Moses, when he had grown up, refused to be known as the son of Pharaoh's daughter. He chose to be illtreated along with the people of God rather than to enjoy the pleasures of sin for a short time. He regarded disgrace for the sake of Christ as of greater value than the treasures of Egypt, because he was looking ahead to his reward. By faith he left Egypt, not fearing the king's anger; he persevered because he saw him who is invisible"* (Heb. 11:24-27).

We should have Job's kind of integrity. *"I know that my Redeemer lives and that in the end He will stand upon the earth"* (Job 19:25).

We should act on what is revealed. *"In the first year of Darius son of Xerxes (a Mede by descent), who was made ruler over the Babylonian kingdom—in the first year of his reign, I, Daniel, understood from the Scriptures, according to the word of the Lord given to Jeremiah the prophet, that the desolation of Jerusalem would last seventy years. So I turned to the Lord God and pleaded with Him in prayer and petition, in fasting, and in sackcloth and ashes"* (Dan. 9:1-3). *"The secret things belong to the Lord our God, but the things revealed belong to us and to our children forever, that we may follow all the words of this law"* (Deut. 29:29).

We should keep the prophetic message. Paul instructed to hold fast the prophesies he has received, *"Timothy, my son, I give you this instruction in keeping with the prophecies once made about you, so that by following them you may fight the good fight, holding on to faith and a good conscience. Some have rejected these and so have shipwrecked their faith"* (1 Tim. 1:18-19).

We should believe the prophecies that are given to us. *"Believe in the Lord your God* [general prophecies] *and you shall be established; believe His prophets* [personal prophecies], *and you shall prosper"* (2 Chron. 20:20b NKJV).

We should mediate on the words of God. *"Do not let this Book of the Law depart from your mouth; meditate on it day and night, so that you may be careful to do everything written in it. Then you will be prosperous and successful"* (Josh. 1:8).

DECLARATIONS

"Thou shalt also decree a thing, and it shall be established unto thee..." (Job 22:28 KJV).

1. My Lord is ruler of all the world. He is full of justice and goodness always.

   "The earth is the Lord's and everything in it, the world, and all who live in it; for He founded it upon the seas and established it upon the waters" (Psalm 24:1-2).

   "And my God will meet all your needs according to His glorious riches in Christ Jesus" (Philippians 4:19).

   "Surely goodness and love will follow me all the days of my life, and I will dwell in the house of the Lord forever" (Psalm 23:6).

2. All things will go well with me as I believe that He will provide for all my needs, even my soul.

   "But remember the Lord your God, for it is he who gives you the ability to produce wealth, and so confirms his covenant, which he swore to your forefathers, as it is today" (Deuteronomy 8:18).

   "Dear friends, I pray that you may enjoy good health and that all may go well with you, even as your soul is getting along well" (3 John 2).

   "You will be blessed more than any other people; none of your men or women will be childless, nor any of your livestock without young. The Lord will keep you free from every disease. He will not inflict on you the horrible diseases you knew in Egypt, but He will inflict them on all who hate you" (Deuteronomy 7:14-15).

"The fruit of your womb will be blessed, and the crops of your land and the young of your livestock—the calves of your herds and the lambs of your flocks" (Deuteronomy 28:4).

3. My life will be full and my home abundant because I have faith in His promises to me.

    "The Lord will grant you abundant prosperity—in the fruit of your womb, the young of your livestock and the crops of your ground—in the land He swore to your forefathers to give you" (Deuteronomy 28:11).

    "and none will miscarry or be barren in your land. I will give you a full life span" (Exodus 23:26).

    "May the Lord make you increase, both you and your children" (Psalm 115:14).

    "Your wife will be like a fruitful vine within your house; your sons will be like olive shoots round your table" (Psalm 128:3).

    "Being fully persuaded that God had power to do what He had promised" (Romans 4:21).

    "For no matter how many promises God has made, they are 'Yes' in Christ. And so through Him the 'Amen' is spoken by us to the glory of God" (2 Corinthians 1:20).

Chapter 10

REGAINING THE
DESOLATE INHERITANCE

TO BE *DESOLATE* MEANS TO BE LAID WASTE, to be left alone, to be forsaken or abandoned, or to be made barren. Therefore *desolate inheritance* is the blessing or gifting that has *lapsed into idleness* or disuse or any other forms of waste or abandonment. Desolation of an inheritance could be as a result of generational lapse or judgmental suspension from the rights and benefits of the blessing or inheritance. For instance, when Israelites went into Babylonian captivity, their rights and benefits of the inheritance of the Promised Land were suspended for seventy years. This is how the Bible recorded that Jerusalem was desolate for the period that the Israelites were in Babylonian captivity: *"In the first year of Darius son of Xerxes (a Mede by descent), who was made ruler over the Babylonian kingdom—in the first year of his reign, I, Daniel, understood from the Scriptures, according to the word of the Lord given to Jeremiah the prophet, **that the desolation of Jerusalem would last seventy years. So I turned to the Lord God and pleaded with Him in prayer and petition, in fasting, and in sackcloth and ashes"** (Dan. 9:1-3).*

When a blessing in a family line *falls into idleness* or disuse, it becomes desolate. If the desolation was a result of an enemy act in the bloodline, you can obtain that blessing denied the ancestors and by so doing bring justice to the injustice done in the past. The gifts of God are not revocable so any blessings released to your family, but for one reason or another was not used or went into judgmental suspension, are available to you and you can walk into such blessing or inheritance. Because of the duality of existence or operation of blessing or an inheritance, it can slip into desolation in a way that it may not be recognized. This could happen as a result of failure to walk in the knowledge of God by the ancestors or as a result of another form of generational iniquities. You can rise up above all these things and pull these blessings into the reality of your life if the conditions are appropriately met.

Elisha's mantle of prophetic anointing became desolate for a period of time. This is how it happened. Before Elijah died he had to drop his mantle for Elisha to pick up, so that Elisha could continue that earthly assignment. Elijah could not take the mantle to Heaven because it was given for service on the earth and that was irrevocable. Unfortunately, on the part of Elisha, he failed to pass on the gift of this anointing. Like Elijah before him, Elisha could not take the mantle of that gifted anointing back to Heaven. So it rested on his bones after his death. For a while that great anointing became desolate. However, when an unknown person was accidentally dropped in a grave containing the bones of Elisha, the dead body of the unknown person touched the bones of Elisha, and the dead man was revived from death to life.

Desolate inheritance is the blessing or gifting that has
lapsed into idleness or disuse or any other forms
of waste or abandonment.

I believe that the transference of that anointing was so powerful that it brought a dead man to life: *"Elisha died and was buried. Now Moabite raiders used to enter the country every spring. Once while some Israelites were burying a man, suddenly they saw a band of raiders; so they threw the man's body into Elisha's tomb. When **the body touched Elisha's bones, the man came to life and stood up on his feet"*** (2 Kings 13:20-21).

In another instance, the estate and "bishoprick" (office) of Judas Iscariot became desolate. The Bible says, *"For he was numbered with us and had obtained part of this ministry*" (Acts 1:17 KJV). His part of the ministry became desolate: *"For it is written in the book of Psalms, let his habitation* [inheritance in the ministry] *be desolate and let no man dwell therein: And his **bishoprick let another take**"* (Acts 1:20 KJV).

In the same way, there are inheritances today that could be referred to as desolate because they are lying idle. These are the gifts or the anointings of previous generations that are lying idle in the spirit realm that could be appropriated by the present generation for service in the Kingdom of God realm.

In the same principle, Isaac redug the well of Abraham: *"So Isaac moved away from there and encamped in the Valley of Gerar and settled there. Isaac reopened the wells that had been dug in the time of his father Abraham, which the Philistines had stopped up after Abraham died, and he gave them the same names his father had given them. Isaac's servants dug in the valley and discovered a well of fresh water there. But the herdsmen of Gerar quarrelled with Isaac's herdsmen and said, 'The water is ours!' So he named the well Esek, because they disputed with him. Then they dug another well, but they quarrelled over that one also; so he named it Sitnah. He moved on from there and dug another well, and no one quarrelled over it. He named it Rehoboth, saying, 'Now the Lord has given us room and we will flourish in the land'"* (Gen. 26:17-22).

Naboth's name is mentioned in the Bible because he contended for his inheritance. This is what he said, *"The Lord forbid that I should give you the inheritance of my fathers"* (1 Kings 21:3).

Here are two types of desolate inheritance.

1. When an inheritance or blessing has not been used in the natural realm at all and has not been used by the past generation, it still exists in the realm of the spirit. Unused potentials in a family fall into this category of desolate inheritance. The most common cause of this type of desolation is lack of the knowledge of the Triune God, even though great giftedness exists in the family. The right person can appropriate it by fulfilling the conditions for entering into the inheritance. Most often the process involves redemption by the blood of Jesus Christ (salvation) and coming to the personal knowledge of Jesus Christ if the person is not born-again, repentance of the sins of the past and present

generations, prayers, fasting and training, and equipping for the work of the ministry.

Adam brought the curse upon humankind and Jesus broke the curse and replaced it with blessing for those redeemed by His blood.

2. When the inheritance or blessing has been walked in by someone in the past generation but has fallen into disuse thereafter. In most cases even certain levels of spiritual maturity may have been attained in the use of the gift. This type of desolate inheritance can be regained, and the family can move in an accelerated pace toward the already acquired level of spiritual maturity that existed in the previous generation.

Biblical passages relevant to this principle of transference of blessings or curses through the generation:

> *But the gift is not like the trespass. For if the many died by the trespass of the one man, how much more did God's grace and the gift that came by the grace of the one man, Jesus Christ, overflow to the many! Again, the gift of God is not like the result of the one man's sin: The judgment followed one sin and brought condemnation, but the gift followed many trespasses and brought justification. For if, by the trespass of the one man, death reigned through that one man, how much more will those who receive God's abundant provision of grace and of the gift of righteousness reign in life through the one man, Jesus Christ. Consequently, just as the result of one trespass was condemnation for all men, so also the result of one act of righteousness was justification that brings life for all men. For just as through the disobedience of the one man the many were made sinners, so also through the obedience of the one man the many will be made righteous* (Romans 5:15-19).

> *This man, however, did not trace his descent from Levi, yet he collected a tenth from Abraham and blessed him who had the promises. And without doubt the lesser person is blessed by the greater. In the one case, the tenth is collected by men who die; but in the other case, by him who is declared to be living. One might even say that Levi, who*

collects the tenth, paid the tenth through Abraham, because when Melchizedek met Abraham, Levi was still in the body of his ancestor (Hebrews 7:6-10).

Steps to Obtain Your Desolate Inheritance

1. Seek the details about any blessing that has become desolate; ask God for His will regarding the blessing and plead that He might use you: *"So Manoah asked him, 'When your words **are fulfilled**, what is to be **the rule for the boy's life** and **work?**' The angel of the Lord answered, 'Your wife must do all that I have told her'* (Judges 13:12-13).

Here we see how God visited the family of Manoah with a promise to end the desolation of Israel and how the family rightly requested the rules of life for entering into that inheritance.

2. Find the reason for the desolation, then repent, purify, and sanctify yourself and others in readiness. Make appropriate restitution: *"In the first year of Darius son of Xerxes (a Mede by descent), who was made ruler over the Babylonian kingdom—in the first year of his reign, I, Daniel, understood from the Scriptures, according to the word of the Lord given to Jeremiah the prophet, that the desolation of Jerusalem would last seventy years. So I turned to the Lord God and pleaded with Him in prayer and petition, in fasting, and in sackcloth and ashes"* (Daniel 9:1-3).

Notice the sequence of events in Daniel's bid to recover Israel's desolate inheritance. Daniel:

- Made an intensive search for the reason for the desolation.
- Discovered the reason for the desolation and the extent of the desolation, together with the magnitude of the prescribed punishment.
- Humbled himself in prayers and fasting.
- Confessed the sins of his ancestors and also for his generation.

While I was speaking and praying, confessing my sin and the sin of my people Israel and making my request to the Lord my God for His holy hill—while I was still in prayer, Gabriel, the man I had seen in the earlier vision, came to me in swift flight about the time of the evening sacrifice. He instructed me and said to me, "Daniel, I have now come to give you insight and understanding. As soon as you began to pray, an answer was given, which I have come to tell you, for you are highly esteemed. Therefore, consider the message and understand the vision" (Daniel 9:20-23).

Notice from the passage in Daniel that:

- The Lord heard as Daniel's words came up to Heaven.
- The Lord made appropriate response from His heavenly abode.

Sometimes in the history of Israel, the people experienced severe famine for three consecutive years. When King David discovered the reason for their problem he made the required restitution and the curse on the land was lifted and that brief suspension from the benefits of the Promised Land was ended.

During the reign of David, there was a famine for three successive years; so David sought the face of the Lord. The Lord said, "It is on account of Saul and his blood-stained house; it is because he put the Gibeonites to death." The king summoned the Gibeonites and spoke to them. (Now the Gibeonites were not a part of Israel but were survivors of the Amorites; the Israelites had sworn to spare them, but Saul in his zeal for Israel and Judah had tried to annihilate them.) David asked the Gibeonites, "What shall I do for you? How shall I make amends so that you will bless the Lord's inheritance?" The Gibeonites answered him, "We have no right to demand silver or gold from Saul or his family, nor do we have the right to put anyone in Israel to death." "What do you want me to do for you?" David asked. They answered the king, "As for the man who destroyed us and plotted against us so that we have been decimated and have no place anywhere in Israel, let seven of his male descendants be given to us to be killed and exposed before the Lord at Gibeah of Saul—the Lord's chosen one." So the king said, "I will give them to you" (2 Samuel 21:1-6).

Josiah made dramatic reform when he discovered and read the warning on the book of law. Josiah was a boy king; he was eight years old when he became the king of Judah. The book of the law was discovered in his days and when it was certified authentic and read to him, he responded with a remarkable depth of commitment, tore his robes in shame, and pledged himself and the entire nation to the terms of the covenant contained in the book of law. He then led the nation into one of the most dramatic reform movements in the history of Judah.

> *In the eighteenth year of his reign, King Josiah sent the secretary, Shaphan son of Azaliah, the son of Meshullam, to the temple of the Lord. He said: "Go up to Hilkiah the high priest and make him get ready the money that has been brought into the temple of the Lord, which the doorkeepers have collected from the people. Make them entrust it to the men appointed to supervise the work on the temple. And make these men pay the workers who repair the temple of the Lord—the carpenters, the builders and the masons. Also make them purchase timber and dressed stone to repair the temple. But they need not account for the money entrusted to them, because they are acting faithfully." Hilkiah the high priest said to Shaphan the secretary, "I have found the Book of the Law in the temple of the Lord." He gave it to Shaphan, who read it. Then Shaphan the secretary went to the king and reported to him: "Your officials have paid out the money that was in the temple of the Lord and have entrusted it to the workers and supervisors at the temple." Then Shaphan the secretary informed the king, "Hilkiah the priest has given me a book." And Shaphan read from it in the presence of the king. When the king heard the words of the Book of the Law, he tore his robes* (2 Kings 22:3-11).

3. Equip yourself and others for the specific assignment connected to the blessing. King Hezekiah is remembered among other reasons as one of the greatest revivalists in the Old Testament. When he discovered the desolation of his people, he carried out purification, sanctification, and consecration of the temple and the priesthood.

In the first month of the first year of his reign, he opened the doors of the temple of the Lord and repaired them. He brought in the priests and the Levites, assembled them in the square on the east side and said, "Listen to me, Levites! Consecrate yourselves now and consecrate the temple of the Lord, the God of your fathers. Remove all defilement from the sanctuary. Our fathers were unfaithful; they did evil in the eyes of the Lord our God and forsook him. They turned their faces away from the Lord's dwelling place and turned their backs on Him. They also shut the doors of the portico and put out the lamps. They did not burn incense or present any burnt offerings at the sanctuary to the God of Israel. Therefore, the anger of the Lord has fallen on Judah and Jerusalem; He has made them an object of dread and horror and scorn, as you can see with your own eyes. This is why our fathers have fallen by the sword and why our sons and daughters and our wives are in captivity. Now I intend to make a covenant with the Lord, the God of Israel, so that His fierce anger will turn away from us. My sons, do not be negligent now, for the Lord has chosen you to stand before Him and serve Him, to minister before Him and to burn incense" (2 Chronicles 29:3-11).

When the offerings were finished, the king and everyone present with him knelt down and worshiped. King Hezekiah and his officials ordered the Levites to praise the Lord with the words of David and of Asaph the seer. So they sang praises with gladness and bowed their heads and worshiped (2 Chronicles 29:29-30).

4.   Ensure there are no compromises in fulfilling the plans of God. Joshua did not completely eradicate the remnant of the Gath tribe as prescribed by God and that mistake later became a reproach to the nation of Israel; *"No Anakites were left in Israelite territory; only in Gaza, Gath and Ashdod did any survive"* (Josh. 11:22).

And out of this small remnant came the giant Goliath.

A champion named Goliath, who was from Gath, came out of the Philistine camp. He was over nine feet tall. He had a bronze helmet on his head and wore a coat of scale armour of bronze weighing five thousand shekels; on his legs he wore bronze greaves, and a bronze javelin was slung on his back. His spear shaft was like a weaver's rod, and its iron point weighed six hundred shekels. His shield-bearer went ahead of him. Goliath stood and shouted to the ranks of Israel, "Why do you come out and line up for battle? Am I not a Philistine, and are you not the servants of Saul? Choose a man and have him come down to me. If he is able to fight and kill me, we will become your subjects; but if I overcome him and kill him, you will become our subjects and serve us." Then the Philistine said, "This day I defy the ranks of Israel! Give me a man and let us fight each other." On hearing the Philistine's words, Saul and all the Israelites were dismayed and terrified (1 Samuel 17:4-11).

Now since the Lord, the God of Israel has driven the Amorites out before his people Israel, what right have you to take it over? Will you not take what your god Chemosh gives you? Likewise, whatever the Lord our God has given us, we will possess (Judges 11:23-24).

But Naboth replied, "The Lord forbid that I should give you the inheritance of my fathers." (1 Kings 21:3).

So Joshua took the entire land, just as the Lord had directed Moses, and he gave it as an inheritance to Israel according to their tribal divisions. Then the land had rest from war (Joshua 11:23).

5. Make commitment by public declaration for righteousness as you walk with God regarding the possession of the blessing.

When the Lord your God has brought you into the land you are entering to possess, you are to proclaim on Mount Gerizim the blessings, and on Mount Ebal the curses (Deuteronomy 11:29).

When you make pronouncements publicly, what you say will be witnessed by a great cloud of witnesses in the spirit realm.

DECLARATIONS

"Thou shalt also decree a thing, and it shall be established unto thee..." (Job 22:28 KJV).

1. Lord, I commit my life to You and I seek Your face in keeping me righteous and true to Your commandments.

    "The righteous will flourish like a palm tree, they will grow like a cedar of Lebanon; planted in the house of the Lord, they will flourish in the courts of our God. They will still bear fruit in old age, they will stay fresh and green, proclaiming, 'The Lord is upright; He is my Rock, and there is no wickedness in Him'" (Psalm 92:12-15).

    "and David enquired of the Lord, 'Shall I pursue this raiding party? Will I overtake them?' 'Pursue them,' He answered. 'You will certainly overtake them and succeed in the rescue'" (1 Samuel 30:8).

    "Surely goodness and love will follow me all the days of my life, and I will dwell in the house of the Lord forever" (Psalm 23:6).

2. God, You are the Lord of all the heavens and earth. You are steadfast and worthy to be praised now and forever more.

    "But remember the Lord your God, for it is He who gives you the ability to produce wealth, and so confirms His covenant, which He swore to your forefathers, as it is today" (Deuteronomy 8:18).

    "(The Lord made the Egyptians favorably disposed toward the people, and Moses himself was highly regarded in Egypt by Pharaoh's officials and by the people)" (Exodus 11:3).

    "The Lord will fulfill His purpose for me; your love, O Lord, endures forever—do not abandon the works of Your hands" (Psalm 138:8).

Chapter 11

PASSING THE TORCH

*P*ASSING THE TORCH is a commonly used phrase when the head of a corporation passes on to his successor the staff of the leadership publicly among pomp and pageantry. The second Book of Timothy demonstrates this principle as it relates to the spiritual realm in a unique but special way. As life closes in on the apostle Paul, he reflects and writes from his lonely abandonment to his spiritual son, Timothy. He recalls with emotions the depth of their relationship, his reliance on Timothy, and Timothy's loyalty to the bonds of relationship. Paul also mentions the rich heritage of Timothy from his biological parents and grandmother. Here we see an example of spiritual and biological inheritance working for good in a single individual.

> *I have been reminded of your sincere faith, which **first lived in your grandmother Lois** and in **your mother Eunice** and, I am persuaded, **now lives in you also**. For this reason I remind you to fan into flame the gift of God, which is in you through **the laying on of my hands** (2 Timothy 1:5-6).*

In this chapter we will explore spiritual DNA and the principles of appropriate exchange of the staff of authority in a ministry (the baton exchange). The staff of authority (the baton) in a ministry is better exchanged without allowing the mandate on the ministry to lapse into any form of desolation. Unfortunately despite all human efforts and good intentions, any inheritance can imperceptibly slip into some form of desolation. For most of the time this slip could be so subtle that despite our best guard, it can occur whether or not we notice it. We should therefore make every effort to ensure proper transference of the baton in the ministry, as the saying goes; success without a successor is no success. This process of transference of the baton is not haphazard, and it follows biblical principles. Many ministries have suffered temporary shipwreck or even permanent shipwreck as in the case of Priest Eli when there was a wrong exchange of baton to his sons. Many people may find it hard to comprehend the process, but there seems to be strict spiritual principles guiding this process that we all need to understand.

This process of transference of the baton in a ministry is not haphazard, and it follows biblical principles.

THE DNA SYSTEMS

Appropriate understanding of the principles of exchange of the staff of authority in a ministry is predicated on understanding the dynamics of the spiritual and bloodline DNA systems and how they interact.

There are two types of DNA systems for the transference of inheritance in the ministry: the family DNA system and the spiritual DNA system.

DNA is originally a genetic term used in scientific literature that refers to the unit of transfer of genetic make-up of an organism. DNA is the basis for the transference of characteristics and similarity in traits from an organism to progeny. Recently, however, the term has found another use in spiritual literature. When used in the spiritual sense, it connotes the unit of transfer of the anointing of a ministry or traits of the particular call of God on an individual or on a ministry.

Spiritual DNA System

I believe that we can begin to understand the principles of spiritual DNA if we study closely what God said to the prophet Jeremiah: *"Now the word of the Lord came to me saying,* **before I formed you in the womb**, *I knew you. And before you were borne I consecrated you; I have appointed you a prophet to the nations"* (Jer. 1:4-5).

This Scripture passage is a reflection of spiritual DNA, which God spoke into humankind, and it exists at an individual level in every person. In every person spiritual DNA predates the *coming together* of bloodline DNA system. The term *formed* in the womb refers to bloodline DNA. My conclusion is that the spiritual DNA system precedes the bloodline DNA system, that is, before the forming of the body. The Lord *knew and ordained* Jeremiah before his body was formed. This in my mind is the essence of the spiritual DNA system.

Bloodline, or Family, DNA System

I believe we can begin to gain some understanding of the bloodline DNA system from the words of the Psalmist, *"For You created my inmost being;* **You knit me together in my mother's womb**. *I praise You because I am fearfully and wonderfully made; Your works are wonderful, I know that full well. My frame was not hidden from You when I was made in the secret place. When I was woven together in the depths of the earth, Your eyes saw my unformed body. All the days ordained for me were written in Your book before one of them came to be"* (Ps. 139:13-16).

In the words of the Psalmist, the knitting together in the mother's womb refers to what I call bloodline DNA. This system follows blood related or biological principle for sonship. Whereas the spiritual DNA system follows spiritual principles, when the two systems are properly blended together and used under God's guidance, they do not conflict.

In every person spiritual DNA predates the *coming together* of bloodline DNA system.

The expression of the bloodline DNA is influenced by many factors in life but the spiritual DNA is probably connected with the eternity placed in the heart of man and only God and the person can reach it. *"He has made everything beautiful in its time. He has also set eternity in the hearts of men, yet they cannot fathom what God has done from the beginning to end"* (Eccl. 3:11).

ACTIVATING YOUR SPIRITUAL DNA SYSTEM

Our interaction with the world system is via the expression of our bloodline DNA system but God always speaks to our potentials inherent in our spiritual DNA to lead us to our destiny. As we pass through life, the bloodline DNA system, by expression or manifestation, may want to overshadow or even try to deny our spiritual DNA. The onus is on us to continuously keep our spiritual DNA in tune with the plans of God. King David must have had this in mind and also the apostle Paul must have wrestled with this tendency when he said, *"For what I do is not the good I want to do; no, the evil I do not want to do—this I keep on doing. Now if I do what I do not want to do, it is no longer I who do it, but it is sin living in me that does it. So I find this law at work: When I want to do good, evil is right there with me. For in my inner being I delight in God's law; but I see another law at work in the members of my body, waging war against the law of my mind and making me a prisoner of the law of sin at work within my members. What a wretched man I am! Who will rescue me from this body of death? Thanks be to God—through Jesus Christ our Lord! So then, I myself in my mind am a slave to God's law, but in the sinful nature a slave to the law of sin"* (Rom. 7:19-25).

This is how King David overcame the evil consequences that emanated from the weakness inherent in his biological DNA system. He sought the reactivation of his spiritual DNA system to bring himself in alignment with his divine destiny.

Cleanse me with hyssop, and I shall be clean; wash me, and I shall be whiter than snow. Let me hear joy and gladness; let the bones You have crushed rejoice. Hide Your face from my sins and blot out all my iniquity. Create in me a pure heart, O God, and renew a steadfast spirit within me. Do not cast me from Your presence or take Your Holy

*Spirit from me. Restore to me the joy of Your salvation and grant me
a willing spirit, to sustain me (Psalm 51:7-12).*

*When I kept silent, my bones wasted away through my groaning
all day long. For day and night Your hand was heavy upon me; my
strength was sapped as in the heat of summer. Selah Then I acknowl-
edged my sin to You and did not cover up my iniquity. I said, "I will
confess my transgressions to the Lord"—and You forgave the guilt of
my sin. Selah (Psalm 32:3-5).*

WHEN GOD ACTIVATES YOUR SPIRITUAL DNA

Sometimes God Himself may come to us in the midst of our weakness and
worldly pursuit and speak to our spirit about the inherent spiritual DNA to bring
us into alignment with the purposes of God in our lives. We see this process twice
in the life of Jacob.

Jacob was running away from the consequences of his bloodline trait of deception when God appeared to him at Bethel and again at the Ford of Jabbok.

1. Jacob and the ladder to heaven. *"Jacob left Beersheba and set out for Haran.
When he reached a certain place, he stopped for the night because the sun had set. Taking one of the stones there, he put it under his head and lay down to sleep. He had a
dream in which he saw a stairway resting on the earth, with its top reaching to heaven,
and the angels of God were ascending and descending on it. There above it stood the
Lord, and He said: "I am the Lord, the God of your father Abraham and the God
of Isaac. I will give you and your descendants the land on which you are lying. Your
descendants will be like the dust of the earth, and you will spread out to the west and to
the east, to the north and to the south. All peoples on earth will be blessed through you
and your offspring. I am with you and will watch over you wherever you go, and I will
bring you back to this land. I will not leave you until I have done what I have promised
you"* (Gen. 28:10-15).

2. Jacob wrestled with an angel of the Lord. *"That night Jacob got up and took
his two wives, his two maidservants and his eleven sons and crossed the ford of the*

Jabbok. After he had sent them across the stream, he sent over all his possessions. So Jacob was left alone, and a man wrestled with him till daybreak. When the man saw that he could not overpower him, He touched the socket of Jacob's hip so that his hip was wrenched as he wrestled with the man. Then the man said, 'Let Me go, for it is daybreak.' But Jacob replied, 'I will not let You go unless You bless me.' The man asked him, 'What is your name?' 'Jacob,' he answered. Then the man said, 'Your name will no longer be Jacob, but Israel, because you have struggled with God and with men and have overcome' (Gen. 32:22-28).

Apostle Paul, then known as Saul of Tarsus, was on collision course with the early church when God apprehended him on his way to Damascus: *"Meanwhile, Saul was still breathing out murderous threats against the Lord's disciples. He went to the high priest and asked him for letters to the synagogues in Damascus, so that if he found any there who belonged to the Way, whether men or women, he might take them as prisoners to Jerusalem. As he neared Damascus on his journey, suddenly a light from heaven flashed around him. He fell to the ground and heard a voice say to him, 'Saul, Saul, why do you persecute Me?' 'Who are You, Lord?' Saul asked. 'I am Jesus, whom you are persecuting,' he replied. 'Now get up and go into the city, and you will be told what you must do.' The men traveling with Saul stood there speechless; they heard the sound but did not see anyone. Saul got up from the ground, but when he opened his eyes he could see nothing. So they led him by the hand into Damascus. For three days he was blind, and did not eat or drink anything"* (Acts 9:1-9).

EXCHANGE OF THE STAFF OF AUTHORITY BIBLICAL EXAMPLES

BATON EXCHANGE	DNA SYSTEM INVOLVED	COMMENTS
David / Solomon	Family with Spiritual DNA	Family DNA must be backed by spiritual DNA to be effective.
		1 Chronicles 28:5—*Of all my sons—and the Lord has given me many—he has chosen my son Solomon to sit on the throne of the kingdom of the Lord over Israel.*
David / Hezekiah	Spiritual DNA	Spiritual DNA can stand alone.
		2 Kings 18:3-4—*He did what was right in the eyes of the Lord, **just as his father David had done.** He removed the high places, smashed the sacred stones and cut down the Asherah poles. He broke into pieces the bronze snake Moses had made, for up to that time the Israelites had been burning incense to it. (It was called Nehushtan.)*
David / Jesus Christ	Spiritual DNA	**Mark 10:47**—*When he heard that it was Jesus of Nazareth, he began to shout, "Jesus, Son of David, have mercy on me!"*
Eli / his sons	Family DNA without Spiritual DNA	Family DNA alone for the basis of transference of the staff of authority is insufficient.
		1 Samuel 3:11-13—*And the Lord said to Samuel:"See, I am about to do something in Israel that will make the ears of everyone who hears of it tingle. At that time I will carry out against Eli everything I spoke against his family—from beginning to end. For I told him that I would judge his family forever because of the sin he knew about; his sons made themselves contemptible, and he failed to restrain them."*

BATON EXCHANGE	DNA SYSTEM INVOLVED	COMMENTS
Eli / Samuel	Spiritual DNA without Family DNA	Can stand alone. **1 Samuel 3:1** — *The boy Samuel ministered before the Lord under Eli. In those days the word of the Lord was rare; there were not many visions.* See also 1 Samuel 3:19-21.
Judas Iscariot / Matthias	None	Democratic decision. They did not wait as they were told to for the promised Holy Spirit. Matthias' election to replace Judas Iscariot as the twelfth disciple was the first and last time we heard about him. **Acts 1:21-26** — *"Therefore it is necessary to choose one of the men who have been with us the whole time the Lord Jesus went in and out among us, beginning from John's baptism to the time when Jesus was taken up from us. For one of these must become a witness with us of his resurrection." So they proposed two men: Joseph called Barsabbas (also known as Justus) and Matthias. Then they prayed, "Lord, You know everyone's heart. Show us which of these two You have chosen to take over this apostolic ministry, which Judas left to go where he belongs." Then they cast lots, and the lot fell to Matthias; so he was added to the eleven apostles.*
Elijah / Elisha	Spiritual DNA	Spiritual DNA can stand alone. **1 Kings 19:16** — *Also, anoint Jehu son of Nimshi king over Israel, and anoint Elisha son of Shaphat from Abel Meholah to succeed you as prophet.*

BATON EXCHANGE	DNA SYSTEM INVOLVED	COMMENTS
Elisha / Gehazi	None	The rod of Elisha did not flourish in the hands of Gehazi. Gehazi forfeited his inheritance.
		2 Kings 4:29-31—*Elisha said to Gehazi, "Tuck your cloak into your belt, take my staff in your hand and run. If you meet anyone, do not greet him, and if anyone greets you, do not answer. Lay my staff on the boy's face." But the child's mother said, "As surely as the Lord lives and as you live, I will not leave you." So he got up and followed her. Gehazi went on ahead and laid the staff on the boy's face, but there was no sound or response. So Gehazi went back to meet Elisha and told him, "The boy has not awakened."*
		2 Kings 5:26-27—*But Elisha said to him, "Was not my spirit with you when the man got down from his chariot to meet you? Is this the time to take money, or to accept clothes, olive groves, vineyards, flocks, herds, or menservants and maidservants? Naaman's leprosy will cling to you and to your descendants forever." Then Gehazi went from Elisha's presence and he was leprous, as white as snow.*

BATON EXCHANGE	DNA SYSTEM INVOLVED	COMMENTS
Moses / Joshua	Spiritual DNA	**Deuteronomy 31:1-3**—*Then Moses went out and spoke these words to all Israel:"I am now a hundred and twenty years old and I am no longer able to lead you. The Lord has said to me, 'You shall not cross the Jordan.' The Lord your God Himself will cross over ahead of you. He will destroy these nations before you, and you will take possession of their land. Joshua also will cross over ahead of you, as the Lord said.*
The mantle of the 12th apostle / Saul of Tarsus	Spiritual DNA	Chosen by God as an apostle to the Gentiles. **Acts 26:15-18**—*"Then I asked, 'Who are you, Lord?' "'I am Jesus, whom you are persecuting,' the Lord replied. 'Now get up and stand on your feet. I have appeared to you to appoint you as a servant and as a witness of what you have seen of Me and what I will show you. I will rescue you from your own people and from the Gentiles. I am sending you to them to open their eyes and turn them from darkness to light, and from the power of Satan to God, so that they may receive forgiveness of sins and a place among those who are sanctified by faith in Me.'*

BASIC KEY FACTS

- God Himself determines to whom and when the exchange should take place.

- From scriptural examples, God usually speaks to the incumbent bearer of the staff of authority regarding the successor; God told Elijah to anoint Elisha as his successor: *"Also, anoint Jehu son of Nimshi king over Israel, and anoint Elisha son of Shaphat from Abel Meholah to succeed you as prophet"* (1 Kings 19:16), and God told Eli about his corrupt sons but Eli did nothing about them and allowed them to continue as priests.

- Often one individual can carry both the family *and* spiritual DNA systems for the ministry.

- Many present-day ministries operating on global scale, because of the God-ordained expansion they have experienced, will give rise to multiple ministries as the anointing can no longer be contained and carried by one person, so inheritance will be split into many different powerful ministries with different batons.

- Family DNA transference usually follows *first-born principles*, but spiritual DNA does not, because it is sovereignly determined. Even when both family DNA and spiritual DNA are operative in a situation, God will sovereignly decide the spiritual DNA component. For example, King Solomon was not the first-born of King David but was chosen by God to be the successor to David by God.

- There is no time or distance barrier to the transference of spiritual DNA. Consider this, the Bible described King Hezekiah as the son of David instead of his biological father, King Ahaz (see 2 Kings 18:3-4). Thus King Hezekiah through righteous living was able to bridge the generational gap and acquired the spiritual DNA of David in that regard. *Jesus is also the son of David both by bloodline and spiritual DNA transference.*

- By sinful living, the benefits of spiritual DNA can be forfeited: *"And the Lord said to Samuel: 'See, I am about to do something in Israel that will make the ears of everyone who hears of it tingle. At that time I will carry out against Eli everything I spoke against his family—from beginning to end. For I told him that I would judge his family for ever because of the sin he knew about; his sons made themselves contemptible, and he failed to restrain them'"* (1 Sam. 3:11-13).

- Spiritual DNA transference is not predicated on human process such as reasoning or democratic process but is totally the prerogative of the sovereign God. Hence Judah, in spite of all his moral failings, was divinely chosen to be the blood lineage for Jesus Christ and not Joseph though he would appear to be better qualified. The eleven apostles chose the replacement for Judas Iscariot but God sovereignly chose Paul as an apostle to the Gentiles.

- There is always a price to pay to receive the benefits of spiritual DNA as Elisha demonstrated: *"When they had crossed, Elijah said to Elisha, "Tell me, what can I do for you before I am taken from you?" "Let me inherit a double portion of your spirit," Elisha replied. "You have asked a difficult thing," Elijah said, "yet if you see me when I am taken from you, it will be yours—otherwise not." As they were walking along and talking together, suddenly a chariot of fire and horses of fire appeared and separated the two of them, and Elijah went up to heaven in a whirlwind. Elisha saw this and cried out, "My father! My father! The chariots and horsemen of Israel!" And Elisha saw him no more. Then he took hold of his own clothes and tore them apart. He picked up the cloak that had fallen from Elijah and went back and stood on the bank of the Jordan. Then he took the cloak that had fallen from him and struck the water with it. "Where now is the Lord, the God of Elijah?" he asked. When he struck the water, it divided to the right and to the left, and he crossed over. The company of the prophets from Jericho, who were watching, said, "The spirit of Elijah is resting on Elisha." And they went to meet him and bowed to the ground before him"* (2 Kings 2:9-15).

- The staff authority will not flourish in the hands of a corrupt son, whether bloodline or spiritual: *"Elisha said to Gehazi, 'Tuck your cloak into your belt, take my staff in your hand and run. If you meet anyone, do not greet him, and if anyone greets you, do not answer. Lay my staff on the boy's face.' But the child's mother said, 'As surely as the Lord lives and as you live, I will not leave you.' So he got up and followed her. Gehazi went on ahead and laid the staff on the boy's face, but there was no sound or response. So Gehazi went back to meet Elisha and told him, 'The boy has not awakened'"* (2 Kings 4:29-31). The rod of Elisha did not flourish in the hands of Gehazi.

- The incumbent baton bearer can often *test the readiness* of a son to inherit the staff of authority because it will not flourish under his supervision if the son is not ready. Elisha gave his staff of authority to Gehazi as in the previous Scripture passage and the staff did not flourish. *"Gehazi went on ahead and laid the staff on the boy's face, but there was no sound or response. So Gehazi went back to meet Elisha and told him, 'The boy has not awakened'"* (2 Kings 4:31).

There are many instances in our generation to bear credence to this phenomenon: Billy Graham's son has stepped into his father's ministry; and Joel Osteen, who has one of the largest congregations in the world, is moving at spiritual maturity well beyond his years because his father made the sacrifice and laid a strong foundation for his family. Joel Osteen and others like him have not relented in their efforts to see their dreams realized. These examples carry both the biological and spiritual DNA systems of the staff of authority in their ministries. And no doubt Pastor Benny Hinn will rejoice when his children walk into the many various aspects of his ministry.

DECLARATIONS

"Thou shalt also decree a thing, and it shall be established unto thee..."
(Job 22:28 KJV).

1. O God, answer my prayers and let the people know that You are God.

   "At the time of sacrifice, the prophet Elijah stepped forward and prayed: 'O Lord, God of Abraham, Isaac and Israel, let it be known today that You are God in Israel and that I am Your servant and have done all these things at Your command. Answer me, O Lord, answer me, so these people will know that You, O Lord, are God, and that You are turning their hearts back again'" (1 Kings 18:36-37).

   "Answer me quickly, O Lord; my spirit fails. Do not hide Your face from me or I will be like those who go down to the pit" (Psalm 143:7).

2. O Lord! In You I hide myself; drive out the enemies before me and destroy all who incense against me.

   "The bolts of your gates will be iron and bronze, and your strength will equal your days. There is no-one like the God of Jeshurun, who rides on the heavens to help you and on the clouds in His majesty. The eternal God is your refuge, and underneath are the everlasting arms. He will drive out your enemy before you, saying, 'Destroy him!'" (Deuteronomy 33:25-27).

Part III

HOW
TO
WORK
AND
COOPERATE
WITH
ANGELS

INTRODUCTION

OVER A DECADE AGO, God spoke to me about the ministry of angels. I came out of that encounter with God with a burning desire to learn more about angels and how to work with them. Perhaps that formed the basis and audacity for writing this part of the book. As I have done in most of my other writings, I have relied heavily on scriptural examples to explain spiritual principles. This is because I believe that the Word of God brings illumination ("the entrance of the Word brings light") sharper than a two-edged sword and can bring different meanings on different occasions ("once has He spoken, twice have I heard"). I have used personal examples only when it brings a "now" relevance to scriptural examples.

I recall clearly many years ago when God instructed me to start writing and teaching on the ministry of angels. This was my encounter. In this vision as I was lying down, I could see a group of evil people—very cruel people—attack another group of people and stripped them of everything they had. While in the dream, my spirit was grieved, and I wanted to rise up from my lying position but found it very difficult (difficulty or restriction in movement or inability to speak is one of the signs of demonic presence in a dream or visionary encounter). I eventually managed to get into a sitting position, and then noticed the arrival of a group of angels. I knew they were angels in human form, but I'm not really sure how I knew this. I asked if indeed they were angels; they said yes. I asked them to "attack and kill" the evil attackers. They looked surprised and did nothing. I asked again if they were angels and again they said yes. Then I asked them a second time to kill the attackers and they still did not respond to me.

Then suddenly I realized what was wrong with my communication with them. I said to them, "Oh, you do not *kill* spirits, you *bind* spirits! So bind these evil attackers." The angels reached up to the sky, pulled down thick cords, bound the evil attackers, and took them away. Then I woke up.

God spoke to me later regarding learning more about how to work with angels.

Chapter 12

ANGELS AND THE JUSTICE OF GOD

THE ANGELIC REALM is an integral part of God's arsenal. Angels are agents of God's justice. Throughout the Bible and in the contemporary world we see the ministry of angels intricately involved with the administration of God's justice on earth. It was through the ministry of angels that God brought justice to the corrupt city of Sodom and Gomorrah.

At certain moments in time, fortunes change, history is made, and lives are affected! These are the times in life that the divine interjects into the natural, and may culminate in making what is routine and ordinary into something extra ordinary and supernatural. These moments in life are often called destiny points.

At most destiny point situations, God uses angels. Unfortunately, many people expect to meet angels in a stereotyped pattern. However, this is not always so. Angels do not often appear in white robes. The Bible says, *"Do not forget to entertain strangers, for by so doing some people have entertained angels without knowing it"* (Heb. 13:2).

For Paul, one of these points in his life was through a certain disciple named Ananias in Damascus, for Jacob it happened in a certain place called Bethel, and for Joseph one such point was when he was connected to Pharaoh through a certain prisoner in an Egyptian dungeon. The list is endless, but the point is that you should recognize when you reach a destiny point.

The angelic realm is an integral part of God's arsenal.

One of the features of destiny points is that things just fall into place. As the Psalmist says of such a time, *"Your troops will be willing on your day of battle, arrayed in holy majesty, from the womb of the dawn you will receive the dew of your youth"* (Ps. 110:3). Angels are involved in arranging and rearranging events and circumstances to align us to God's destiny for us.

God can meet us in the most unusual place and communicate through the most unpredictable means. God can make manifest His will to us through diverse ways. That is why the Bible says, *"Be on the alert then, for you do not know the day nor the hour"* [of your visitation] (Matt. 25:13 NASB).

Some years ago during the anniversary of a church in Africa, my wife, who was the editor of the church magazine, was worried because there was a lot of work to be done to successfully complete the publication of the magazine and time was fast running out. At that point, we realized that the whole family would have to get involved in the production. I soon discovered that she had every reason to be troubled, but we took solace in the biblical injunction that "all things are possible to them who believe."

I recall that by the eve of the anniversary celebration, just hours to the official launching of the magazine, the printers reported to us that only a few pages had been printed. These were days before the technology of electronic publishing became common, and most printing was manually done. So we had to distribute the remaining pages to four additional printing companies. I started a circle of shuttles between these places to ensure that none of them failed to complete the assignment. If one of them failed, the whole exercise would fail. Also in those days and in that country, gas stations were not able to meet the demand for fuel for the ever rapidly expanding population of car owners. Most times gasoline supply was rationed to ensure everyone would get a supply of fuel. All I can remember is that I started out with a reasonable quantity of fuel in my car.

After numerous circle shuttles between the printing companies, my car ran out of gas at about 3:00 A.M. As I stood in front of one of the presses feeling confused, helpless, and not knowing what to do, I noticed a man who appeared to be drunk, presumably from a social party nearby. As he walked toward a car, I approached him to ask if he would sell me the gas in his car tank. In those days this was not an unusual practice. I was desperate and was ready to pay whatever price he would demand. After all, judging from his state, I thought he should need some money to recover from the night's escapade. To my surprise he simply laughed, went to his car, brought out a gallon of gas, and would not accept any payment. I was so surprised at this kind gesture that I forgot to ask for his name. He went back to his car and drove off.

With gas in my car, I resumed my circle of shuttles. If any of the printers failed to meet his obligation that night, the magazine would not be launched. True to how things usually happen, as I got to one of the presses, the work had stopped, the printing machines were silent, and the job had not been completed. I was told that one of the engine rods had broken and would need to be welded before the work could resume. At this point, I thought it was time to call it quits.

Then suddenly a car pulled up in front of the house adjacent to the press, and to my utmost surprise, it was the same drunken man. This seemingly drunken man came again to me and asked if I was okay. I told him the story of the broken rod.

Again he laughed and said, "I am a welder, get me the two pieces and I will weld them for you." Now I was wiser, no questions asked. He took the rod away and after 30 minutes came back with a welded rod and would not give me his name or address. The entire printing was completed that night. The magazine was successfully launched at the appointed time.

Who was this man? Was he a drunken man who was loafing about under the influence of alcohol or a ministering agent sent by God to meet me at those specific points? What if I had judged this helper by his appearance? I may never know the answer. But the Lord says, *"He will give His angels charge concerning you, to guard you in all your ways."* Angels are ministering spirits sent to minister to those who are heirs of salvation. Remember, for every one fallen angel, there are at least two righteous angels in the service of the Almighty God.

ANGELS ENSURE THE JUSTICE OF GOD

The multiplicity and diversity of the angelic roles and their capabilities are often beyond the imagination of the human mind. Specifically, angels are involved in the furtherance of the justice of God on earth and in the heavenly realm. When there was a rebellion in Heaven, it was archangel Michael and his angels that brought defeat to the rebels.

Let's look at some instances when angels ensured the justice of God.

When an evil principality withheld the divine messenger sent to Daniel, archangel Michael was dispatched to administer justice to the situation:

> *Then he continued, "Do not be afraid, Daniel. Since the first day that you set your mind to gain understanding and to humble yourself before your God, your words were heard, and I have come in response to them. But the prince of the Persian kingdom resisted me twenty-one days. Then Michael, one of the chief princes, came to help me, because I was detained there with the king of Persia. Now I have come to explain to you what will happen to your people in the future, for the vision concerns a time yet to come"* (Daniel 10:12-14).

> *So he said, "Do you know why I have come to you? Soon I will return to fight against the prince of Persia, and when I go, the prince of Greece will come; but first I will tell you what is written in the Book of Truth. (No one supports me against them except Michael, your prince* (Daniel 10:20-21).

These comments by the angels hint at heavenly warfare, that human beings may not be aware of. Nevertheless such struggles do exist in the spirit realm even though we may not know much about them. Sometimes the delay in obtaining answers to our prayer may be due to happenings in this realm. In these passages we can imagine the roles of angels in the heavenly struggles.

In another instance we see where an angel was involved in ensuring victory for the Israelites:

> *Then the angel of God, who had been traveling in front of Israel's army, withdrew and went behind them. The pillar of cloud also moved from in front and stood behind them, coming between the armies of Egypt and Israel. Throughout the night the cloud brought darkness to the one side and light to the other; so neither went near the other all night long* (Exodus 14:19-20).

The multiplicity and diversity of the angelic roles and their capabilities are often beyond the imagination of the human mind.

> *The two angels arrived at Sodom in the evening, and Lot was sitting in the gateway of the city. When he saw them, he got up to meet them and bowed down with his face to the ground. "My lords," he said, "please turn aside to your servant's house. You can wash your feet and spend the night and then go on your way early in the morning." "No," they answered, "we will spend the night in the square." But he insisted so strongly that they did go with him and entered his house. He prepared a meal for them, baking bread without yeast, and they ate. Before they had gone to bed, all the men from every part of the city of Sodom—both young and old—surrounded the house. They called to Lot, "Where are the men who came to you tonight? Bring them out to us so that we can have sex with them." Lot went outside to meet them and shut the door behind him and said, "No, my friends. Don't do this wicked thing. Look, I have two daughters who have never slept with a man. Let me bring them out to you, and you can do what you like with them. But don't do anything to these men, for they have come under the protection*

of my roof." "Get out of our way," they replied. And they said, "This fellow came here as an alien, and now he wants to play the judge! We'll treat you worse than them." They kept bringing pressure on Lot and moved forward to break down the door. But the men inside reached out and pulled Lot back into the house and shut the door. Then they struck the men who were at the door of the house, young and old, with blindness so that they could not find the door (Genesis 19:1-11).

UNDERSTANDING THE MINISTRY OF ANGELS

The Hebrew *Mal-'akh* and the Greek *aggetos* mean "messengers." Angels are mentioned over 400 times in Scriptures. Angels are spirits and as spirits, they are invisible, powerful, and mostly superhuman.

Angels have fascinated generations from time immemorial. From Genesis to Revelation, the Scriptures speak of the activities of angels in the service of God and man. The writer of Hebrews speaking of the angels says, *"Are not all angels ministering spirits sent to serve those who will inherit salvation?"* (Heb. 1:14). Indeed angels are co-servants with the saints in the service of God and are created by God for His work and also to do His pleasure. God uses angels in a variety of ways such as to bring healing, salvation, comforting, even destruction and death. Primarily, angels are dispatched to minister to the saints of God and they do this by obeying the Word of God. Angels do not do a human's bidding, as most people would want to believe, otherwise churches may have used angelic forces against each other.

The Bible says in Hebrews 2:7 that man is created a little lower than angels; we know that angels have greater mental capacity than man and are superhuman in physical power. We see higher angelic knowledge and power in action when two angels brought flaming destruction upon Sodom and Gomorrah and when a single angel killed 185,000 soldiers of the Assyrian army. Though the human spirit is made in the image and likeness of God, the tripartite man as a single being is limited by the possession of an earthly body, hence is lower than angels in the current dispensation on earth. Angels are spirit beings without earthly bodies, but are capable of materializing with borrowed earthly bodies to become visible in the physical realm. Angels can travel at tremendous speed far exceeding the limits of this physical world. However, they are not omnipresent, omniscient, or omnipotent; therefore they are not gods.

The consequences of not cooperating with angels in the fulfillment of their divine assignment on earth are rampart in the Bible. Zechariah, a high priest and the father of John the Baptist could not speak for months until the naming ceremony of John because he doubted the promise brought to him by the angel Gabriel. Lot's wife became a pillar of salt as a result of disobedience to the instructions given by the angels.

The angelic ministry though formidable is largely an invisible part of the army of God that is involved in a wide variety of roles in the service of God and to the heirs of salvation. As spirits, they are primarily invisible and this reality is demonstrated by the story of Elisha and his servant. The co-existing realm of the unseen army of angels was revealed to Elisha's servant, whose eyes were opened when Elisha prayed for him to see into the spirit realm.

> *When the servant of the man of God got up and went out early the next morning, an army with horses and chariots had surrounded the city. "Oh, my lord, what shall we do?" the servant asked. "Don't be afraid," the prophet answered. "Those who are with us are more than those who are with them." And Elisha prayed, "O Lord, open his eyes so that he may see." Then the Lord opened the servant's eyes, and he looked and saw the hills full of horses and chariots of fire all round Elisha* (2 Kings 6:15-17).

The important thing to note is that the angelic host that Elisha's servant saw was there all the time. The same is true for the innumerable angels that camp around us: *"The angel of the Lord encamps around those who fear Him, and He delivers them"* (Ps. 34:7).

To see angels in the physical realm is the exception rather than the rule. We walk with the angelic force by faith believing the Bible that truly they encamp around us all at all times. They are innumerable and are constantly involved in arranging and rearranging divine plans and appointments for human beings. An angel accompanied Abraham's servant to get a wife for Isaac. I believe angels were involved in divinely arranging appointments for Abraham's servant to meet with Rebecca at the well at the right time, just as Abraham had prayed.

The Lord, the God of heaven, who brought me out of my father's household and my native land and who spoke to me and promised me on oath, saying, "To your offspring I will give this land"—He will send his angel before you so that you can get a wife for my son from there. If the woman is unwilling to come back with you, then you will be released from this oath of mine. Only do not take my son back there.' So the servant put his hand under the thigh of his master Abraham and swore an oath to him concerning this matter. Then the servant took ten of his master's camels and left, taking with him all kinds of good things from his master. He set out for Aram Naharaim and made his way to the town of Nahor. He made the camels kneel down near the well outside the town; it was toward evening, the time the women go out to draw water. Then he prayed, "O Lord, God of my master Abraham, give me success today, and show kindness to my master Abraham. See, I am standing beside this spring, and the daughters of the townspeople are coming out to draw water. May it be that when I say to a girl, 'Please let down your jar that I may have a drink,' and she says, 'Drink, and I'll water your camels too'—let her be the one you have chosen for your servant Isaac. By this I will know that you have shown kindness to my master." Before he had finished praying, Rebecca came out with her jar on her shoulder. She was the daughter of Bethuel son of Milcah, who was the wife of Abraham's brother Nahor. The girl was very beautiful, a virgin; no man had ever lain with her. She went down to the spring, filled her jar and came up again (Genesis 24:7-16).

To see angels in the physical realm is the exception rather than the rule. We walk with the angelic force by faith.

This is not a coincidence but an answer to the prayer of Abraham, the father of faith and father of the patriarchs.

Declarations

"Thou shalt also decree a thing, and it shall be established unto thee..." (Job 22:28 KJV).

1. God grant me a discerning spirit to know the wrong from the right and become more useful in Your Kingdom.

   "Your servant is here among the people You have chosen, a great people, too numerous to count or number. So give Your servant a discerning heart to govern Your people and to distinguish between right and wrong. For who is able to govern this great people of Yours?" (1 Kings 3:8-9).

2. I shall overcome all who come against me in the name of Jesus Christ.

   "David said to the Philistine, 'You come against me with sword and spear and javelin, but I come against you in the name of the Lord Almighty, the God of the armies of Israel, whom you have defied. This day the Lord will hand you over to me, and I'll strike you down and cut off your head. Today I will give the carcasses of the Philistine army to the birds of the air and the beasts of the earth, and the whole world will know that there is a God in Israel'" (1 Samuel 17:45-46).

Chapter 13

THE NATURE
OF ANGELS

THERE HAS BEEN MUCH CONFUSION about the nature of angels. Angels are ministering spirits sent to help those who are heirs of salvation. They were individually created and their creation predates the creation of man. They are spiritual beings and are superhuman in many respects, but as stated previously, they are neither omniscient, omnipresent, or omnipotent. Angels were created from fire and winds while man was made from the dust of the earth and became a living soul by the breath of God.

Though angels may exhibit great strength, they are not gods and should not be worshiped. They have the capability to take on temporal appearances if their assignments warrant so. Since they are to minister to heirs of salvation, their involvement in affairs of this world will be greatly increased in the end time. It is therefore pertinent that we get better acquainted and equipped to appropriately relate to angels. God releases angels on assignment. Some angelic assignments may require human cooperation, in which case the assignment is conditional. Or some earthly assignment may not require input from human beings to be accomplished, in which case it is an unconditional assignment.

A few characteristics, traits, and truths about angels follow.

Angels were created before man.

"To the angel of the church in Laodicea write: These are the words of the Amen, the faithful and true witness, the ruler of God's creation" (Revelation 3:14).

"Where were you when I laid the earth's foundation? Tell me, if you understand. Who marked off its dimensions? Surely you know! Who stretched a measuring line across it? On what were its footings set, or who laid its cornerstone—while the morning stars sang together and all the angels shouted for joy?" (Job 38:4-7)

Angels are part of the supernatural realm created by God.

"For by Him all things were created: things in heaven and on earth, visible and invisible, whether thrones or powers or rulers or authorities; all things were created by Him and for Him. He is before all things, and in Him all things hold together. And He is the head of the body, the church; He is the beginning and the firstborn from among the dead, so that in everything He might have the supremacy" (Colossians 1:16-18).

"You alone are the Lord. You made the heavens, even the highest heavens, and all their starry host, the earth and all that is on it, the seas and all that is in them. You give life to everything, and the multitudes of heaven worship You" (Nehemiah 9:6).

Though angels may exhibit great strength, they are not gods and should not be worshiped.

Angels are "innumerable."

"But you have come to Mount Zion, to the heavenly Jerusalem, the city of the living God. You have come to thousands upon thousands of angels in joyful assembly" (Hebrews 12:22).

Angels have limited power and knowledge.

Angels do not have the same knowledge as God; neither do they know the hour of Christ's return. *"No one knows about that day or hour, not even the angels in heaven, nor the Son, but only the Father. Be on guard! Be alert! You do not know when that time will come"* (Mark 13:32-33).

"No one knows about that day or hour, not even the angels in heaven, nor the Son, but only the Father" (Matthew 24:36).

"It was revealed to them that they were not serving themselves but you, when they spoke of the things that have now been told you by those who have preached the gospel to you by the Holy Spirit sent from heaven. Even angels long to look into these things" (1 Peter 1:12).

Angels do not have the same knowledge as God.

Any angelic message must be judged against the eternal word of God: *"But even if we or an angel from heaven should preach a gospel other than the one we preached to you, let him be eternally condemned!"* (Galatians 1:8)

Angels have superhuman power.

"Praise the Lord, you His angels, you mighty ones who do His bidding, who obey His word" (Psalm 103:20).

"because we are going to destroy this place. The outcry to the Lord against its people is so great that he has sent us to destroy it." So Lot went out and spoke to his sons-in-law, who were pledged to marry his daughters. He said, "Hurry and get out of this place, because the Lord is about to destroy the city!" But his sons-in-law thought he was joking. With the coming of dawn, the angels urged Lot, saying, "Hurry! Take your wife and your two daughters who are here, or you will be swept away when the city is punished." When he hesitated, the men grasped his hand and the hands of his wife and of his two daughters and led them safely out of the city, for the Lord was merciful to them. As soon as they had brought them out, one of them said, "Flee for your lives! Don't look back, and don't stop anywhere in the plain! Flee to the mountains or you will be swept away!" But Lot said to them, "No, my lords, please! Your servant has found favor in your eyes, and you have shown great kindness to me in sparing my life. But I can't flee to the mountains; this disaster will overtake me, and I'll die. Look, here is a town near enough to run to, and it is small. Let me flee to it—it is very small, isn't it? Then my life will be spared." He said to him, "Very well, I will grant this request too; I will not overthrow the town you speak of. But flee there quickly, because I cannot do anything until you reach it." (That is why the town was called Zoar.) By the time Lot reached Zoar, the sun had risen over the land. Then the Lord rained down burning sulphur on Sodom and Gomorrah—from the Lord out of the heavens (Genesis 19:13-24).

"That night the angel of the Lord went out and put to death a hundred and eighty-five thousand men in the Assyrian camp. When the people got up the next morning—there were all the dead bodies!" (2 Kings 19:35)

Angels are everlasting.

Angels don't procreate, so they are everlasting beings. Eternity refers to that which has no beginning and no end. Angels are created beings so they have a beginning.

When angels take on a corporeal appearance for a period of time, they often materialize as males in the Scriptures because God the Father and God the Son are spoken of as males.

THE INDIVIDUALITY OF ANGELS

Individual identity among angels is very restricted in the Scriptures because the focus should not be on angels but on the God who created the angels and the divine assignments they are to accomplish. The lack of names was a safeguard against giving undue honor and worship to these creatures. Angels are dispatched to act in God's name, not in their names.

> *Jacob said, "Please tell me your name." But he replied, "Why do you ask my name?" Then he blessed him there* (Genesis 32:29).

> *Then Manoah enquired of the angel of the Lord, "What is your name, so that we may honor you when your word comes true?" He replied, "Why do you ask my name? It is beyond understanding"* (Judges 13:17-18).

Only two holy angels are named in the Scriptures: *Gabriel,* who seems to be God's special messenger, was mentioned in Daniel 9:21 and Luke 1:19,26. The other is *Michael,* who is described as one of the chief princes (see Daniel 10:13), your prince (see Daniel 10:21), the great prince (see Daniel 12:1) and the archangel (see Jude 9). Michael is a leader of God's army (see Revelation 12:7) and the guardian of Israel (see Daniel 12:1).

COMMUNICATION OF ANGELS

As personalities, angels have the power to communicate with one another: *"If I speak in the tongues of men and of angels, but have not love, I am only a resounding gong or a clanging cymbal"* (1 Cor. 13:1).

Angels can also commune with man:

> *The angel of the Lord asked him, "Why have you beaten your donkey these three times? I have come here to oppose you because your path is a reckless one before me. The donkey saw me and turned away from me these three times. If she had not turned away, I would certainly have killed you by now, but I would have spared her." Balaam said to the angel of the Lord, "I have sinned. I did not realize you were standing in the road to oppose me. Now if you are displeased, I will go back." The angel of the Lord said to Balaam, "Go with the men, but speak only what I tell you." So Balaam went with the princes of Balak* (Numbers 22:32-35).

> *One day at about three in the afternoon he had a vision. He distinctly saw an angel of God, who came to him and said, "Cornelius!" Cornelius stared at him in fear. "What is it, Lord?" he asked. The angel answered, "Your prayers and gifts to the poor have come up as a memorial offering before God. Now send men to Joppa to bring back a man named Simon who is called Peter. He is staying with Simon the tanner, whose house is by the sea." When the angel who spoke to him had gone, Cornelius called two of his servants and a devout soldier who was one of his attendants* (Acts 10:3-7).

ANGEL APPEARANCES

Angels appear in different forms depending upon a number of things, such as:
- Their order of creation.
- The assignment on which they are sent.

- The role that man is expected to play in the fulfillment of their assignment.
- The heavenly glory in which they come to the earth.

The cherubim are exotic and beautiful, and they are covered with precious stones (see Ezekiel 28:13-14).

Seraphim are fiery angels and have six wings—with two they cover their faces, with two they cover their feet, and with two they fly. They epitomize humility and praises in the presence of God (see Isaiah 6:2).

Appearances predicated on earthly assignments include:

- David saw the awesome angel of the Lord at the threshing floor of Araunah.
- Balaam saw the angel with a drawn sword.
- Mary saw the angel Gabriel and was able to communicate with him.
- The prophet Daniel saw the same angel as Mary but was unable to stand in his presence.

The Book of Hebrews says we can entertain angels when they come in human form without our knowing. The angels that went on the clandestine trip to Sodom and Gomorrah went as men to carry the true investigation of the allegations against the city of Sodom. They had to interact with men.

Angels appear in different forms depending
upon a number of things

Angels appear in varying degrees of heavenly glory.

Angels don't always appear in flaming glory; they can come veiled in human form: *"Keep on loving each other as brothers. Do not forget to entertain strangers, for by so doing some people have entertained angels without knowing it"* (Heb. 13:1-2).

However, occasionally angels appear with varying degrees of heavenly glory. The Bible speaks of an angel with the appearance of lightning in which reflected the degree of heavenly glory carried by that angel.

> *After the Sabbath, at dawn on the first day of the week, Mary Magdalene and the other Mary went to look at the tomb. There was a violent earthquake, for an angel of the Lord came down from heaven and, going to the tomb, rolled back the stone and sat on it. His appearance was like lightning, and his clothes were white as snow. The guards were so afraid of him that they shook and became like dead men. The angel said to the women, "Do not be afraid, for I know that you are looking for Jesus, who was crucified. He is not here; He has risen, just as He said. Come and see the place where He lay. Then go quickly and tell His disciples: 'He has risen from the dead and is going ahead of you into Galilee. There you will see Him.' Now I have told you"* (Matthew 28:1-7).

**Angels don't always appear in flaming glory;
they can come veiled in human form.**

In one instance, we see when angel Gabriel appeared to Mary in Luke 1:

> *In the sixth month, God sent the angel Gabriel to Nazareth, a town in Galilee, to a virgin pledged to be married to a man named Joseph, a descendant of David. The virgin's name was Mary. The angel went to her and said, "Greetings, you who are highly favored! The Lord is with you." Mary was greatly troubled at his words and wondered what kind of greeting this might be. But the angel said to her, "Do not be afraid, Mary, you have found favor with God. You will be with child and give birth to a son, and you are to give him the name Jesus. He will be great and will be called the Son of the Most High. The*

Lord God will give Him the throne of His father David, and He will reign over the house of Jacob for ever; His kingdom will never end" (Luke 1:26-33).

On another occasion, this same angel Gabriel appeared with higher level of heavenly glory and Daniel could not stand in his presence,

While I, Daniel, was watching the vision and trying to understand it, there before me stood one who looked like a man. And I heard a man's voice from the Ulai calling, "Gabriel, tell this man the meaning of the vision." As he came near the place where I was standing, I was terrified and fell prostrate. "Son of man," he said to me, "understand that the vision concerns the time of the end." While he was speaking to me, I was in a deep sleep, with my face to the ground. Then he touched me and raised me to my feet. He said: "I am going to tell you what will happen later in the time of wrath, because the vision concerns the appointed time of the end" (Daniel 8:15-17).

The amount of glory angels appear in varies according to the assignment and the degree of human interaction in the assignment. If the assignment requires interaction and discussion with human beings, the glory will be veiled to allow for this to happen. If the assignment is essentially for the purpose of impartation and power expression, they appear with a high degree of heavenly glory. This is to allow for the appropriate level of authority and power to be carried from Heaven for the assignment.

ANGEL ASSIGNMENTS

A vast majority of the angelic forces around us are on divine conditional assignments, which means what they eventually end up accomplishing on our behalf is sometimes dependent on what we say or do, as in the case of the angel that rescued Lot insinuates.

Conditional Assignments

Conditional angelic assignments require the participation of man for completion. Therefore we need to know how to maximize our working relationship with the angels. However, most of the angels on conditional assignments also operate with provisos, as in the case of the angel that rescued Lot. Though he was required to wait for Lot's family to leave the city, he had to use some measure of force to take Lot out of Sodom. Lot delayed for family reasons.

> But Lot said to them, "No, my lords, please! Your servant has found favor in your eyes, and you have shown great kindness to me in sparing my life. But I can't flee to the mountains; this disaster will overtake me, and I'll die. Look, here is a town near enough to run to, and it is small. Let me flee to it—it is very small, isn't it? Then my life will be spared." He said to him, "Very well, I will grant this request too; I will not overthrow the town you speak of. But flee there quickly, because I cannot do anything until you reach it." (That is why the town was called Zoar.) By the time Lot reached Zoar, the sun had risen over the land. Then the Lord rained down burning sulphur on Sodom and Gomorrah—from the Lord out of the heavens. Thus He overthrew those cities and the entire plain, including all those living in the cities—and also the vegetation in the land. But Lot's wife looked back, and she became a pillar of salt (Genesis 19:18-26).

Conditional angelic assignments require the participation of man for completion.

Also notice from the story of Balaam and the donkey, the angel would have killed Balaam if he reached a certain point without repenting of his wrong attitude. It would appear that the angel did not intend to stop Balaam from going on his dubious mission but was only required to ensure he repented of it before he went farther, with instructions from God.

> *Then the Lord opened Balaam's eyes, and he saw the angel of the Lord standing in the road with his sword drawn, so he bowed low and fell facedown. The angel of the Lord asked him, "Why have you beaten your donkey these three times? I have come here to oppose you because your path is a reckless one before me. The donkey saw me and turned away from me these three times. If she had not turned away, I would certainly have killed you by now, but I would have spared her." Balaam said to the angel of the Lord, "I have sinned. I did not realize you were standing in the road to oppose me. Now if you are displeased, I will go back." The angel of the Lord said to Balaam, "Go with the men, but speak only what I tell you." So Balaam went with the princes of Balak* (Numbers 22:31-35).

The angel with a drawn sword that met Joshua by the walls of Jericho was very clear on this point, he was neither for Joshua or against him, but what was to happen next was contingent on the response of Joshua to the presence of the angel.

> *Now when Joshua was near Jericho, he looked up and saw a man standing in front of him with a drawn sword in his hand. Joshua went up to him and asked, "Are you for us or for our enemies?" "Neither," he replied, "but as commander of the army of the Lord I have now come." Then Joshua fell facedown to the ground in reverence, and asked him, "What message does my Lord have for His servant?" The commander of the Lord's army replied, "Take off your sandals, for the place where you are standing is holy." And Joshua did so* (Joshua 5:13-15).

Unconditional Assignments

Unconditional assignments are assignments that angels are to perform that are not contingent on human reaction or cooperation for completion.

Then an angel of the Lord appeared to him, standing at the right side of the altar of incense. When Zechariah saw him, he was startled and was gripped with fear. But the angel said to him: "Do not be afraid, Zechariah; your prayer has been heard. Your wife Elizabeth will bear you a son, and you are to give him the name John" (Luke 1:11-13).

The angel went to her and said, "Greetings, you who are highly favored! The Lord is with you." Mary was greatly troubled at his words and wondered what kind of greeting this might be. But the angel said to her, "Do not be afraid, Mary, you have found favor with God. You will be with child and give birth to a son, and you are to give Him the name Jesus. He will be great and will be called the Son of the Most High. The Lord God will give Him the throne of His father David" (Luke 1:28-32).

Unconditional assignments are assignments that angels are to perform that are not contingent on human reaction or cooperation for completion.

For the Lord Himself will come down from heaven, with a loud command, with the voice of the archangel and with the trumpet call of God, and the dead in Christ will rise first. After that, we who are still alive and are left will be caught up together with them in the clouds to meet the Lord in the air. And so we will be with the Lord forever. Therefore encourage each other with these words (1 Thessalonians 4:16-18).

ANGELS HAVE THE RIGHT OF CHOICE

Angels have the power of personal choice between right and wrong. Many angels out of their own volition joined the rebellion of satan against God.

The sons of God saw that the daughters of men were beautiful, and they married any of them they chose (Genesis 6:2).

For if God did not spare angels when they sinned, but sent them to hell, putting them into gloomy dungeons to be held for judgment (2 Peter 2:4).

And there was war in heaven. Michael and his angels fought against the dragon, and the dragon and his angels fought back. But he was not strong enough, and they lost their place in heaven. The great dragon was hurled down—that ancient serpent called the devil, or Satan, who leads the whole world astray. He was hurled to the earth and his angels with him (Revelation 12:7-9).

ANGELS AND JESUS CHRIST'S EARTHLY MINISTRY

The ministry of Jesus Christ was closely associated with angels. Angel Gabriel announced His conception to the Virgin Mary, angels announced His birth to the shepherds, angels ministered to Him after the forty-day fast and temptation in the wilderness, angels were present at His tomb, at His resurrection, and they were present at His ascension to Heaven. Angels were the first to preach the good news of His resurrection from the dead. Furthermore we are told He will return to earth with the shout of the archangel. The Book of Revelation gives credence to the value of angelic ministry in the overall weaponry of Christ and it begins like this:

The revelation of Jesus Christ, which God gave Him to show His servants what must soon take place. He made it known by sending His angel to His servant John (Revelation 1:1).

Angels must not be worshiped or prayed to.

In Bible days many people misunderstood the ministry of the angels, as Paul mentioned in Colossians 2:18, *"Do not let anyone who delights in false humility and the worship of angels disqualify you for the prize. Such a person goes into great detail about what he has seen, and his unspiritual mind puffs him up with idle notions."*

In Revelation 19:10 apostle John says, *"At this I fell at his feet to worship him. But he said to me, 'Do not do it! I am a fellow servant with you and with your brothers who hold to the testimony of Jesus. Worship God! For the testimony of Jesus is the spirit of prophecy.'"*

This was also reiterated in Revelation 22:8-9, *"I, John, am the one who heard and saw these things. And when I had heard and seen them, I fell down to worship at the feet of the angel who had been showing them to me. But he said to me, 'Do not do it! I am a fellow servant with you and with your brothers the prophets and of all who keep the words of this book. Worship God!'"*

The Church will instruct angels.

Angels will be taught by the church as evidenced by these Scriptures:

His intent was that now, through the church, the manifold wisdom of God should be made known to the rulers and authorities in the heavenly realms (Ephesians 3:10).

For it seems to me that God has put us apostles on display at the end of the procession, like men condemned to die in the arena. We have been made spectacles to the whole universe, to angels as well as to men (1 Corinthians 4:9).

Concerning this salvation, the prophets, who spoke of the grace that was to come to you, searched intently and with the greatest care, trying to find out the time and circumstances to which the Spirit of Christ in them was pointing when he predicted the suffering of Christ and the glories that would follow. It was revealed to them that they were not serving themselves but you, when they spoke of the things that have now been told you by those who have preached the gospel to you, by the Holy Spirit sent from heaven. Even angels long to look into these things (1 Peter 1:10-12).

Angels don't need salvation.

For surely it is not angels He helps, but Abraham's descendants. For this reason He had to be made like the brothers in every way, in order that He might become a merciful and faithful high priest in service to God, and that He might make atonement for the sins of the people (Hebrews 2:16-17).

DECLARATIONS

"Thou shalt also decree a thing, and it shall be established unto thee..." (Job 22:28 KJV).

1. Lord be merciful unto me and let Your compassion surround me for I wait in You and for You.

   "Yet the Lord longs to be gracious to you; He rises to show you compassion. For the Lord is a God of justice. Blessed are all who wait for Him!" (Isaiah 30:18)

2. The rod of the wicked will not rest in my household.

   "Far be it from you to do such a thing—to kill the righteous with the wicked, treating the righteous and the wicked alike. Far be it from you! Will not the Judge of all the earth do right?" (Genesis 18:25)

Chapter 14

THE ROLES AND CATEGORIES OF ANGELS

THE ROLES OF ANGELS

THERE ARE SEVERAL HINTS in the Bible that suggest that there are specific angelic roles. In the Book of Revelation we read that there is an angel in charge of water.

> *The third angel poured out his bowl on the rivers and springs of water, and they became blood. Then I heard the angel in charge of the waters say: "You are just in these judgments, You who are and who were, the Holy One, because You have so judged* (Revelation 16:4-5).

We also read of the angel of Israel.

> *At that time Michael, the great prince who protects your people, will arise. There will be a time of distress such as has not happened from the beginning of nations until then. But at that time your people— everyone whose name is found written in the book—will be delivered. Multitudes who sleep in the dust of the earth will awake: some to everlasting life, others to shame and everlasting contempt. Those who are*

wise will shine like the brightness of the heavens, and those who lead many to righteousness, like the stars for ever and ever. But you, Daniel, close up and seal the words of the scroll until the time of the end. Many will go here and there to increase knowledge (Daniel 12:1-4).

Archangel Michael seems to be connected with warfare while angel Gabriel seems to be connected with bringing news or fresh insight from Heaven to earth. Seraphim are connected with worshiping and the living creatures seem to be connected with transportation.

There may therefore be specific angels in Heaven that are assigned to specific duties.

Angels Build Up the Body of Christ

God's purpose for creating the angels is to build up the Body of Christ. They do this in the following ways:

- *Praise the Lord, you His angels, you mighty ones who do His bidding, who obey His word* (Psalm 103:20).
- By blessing the Lord in worship and in service: *"And again, when God brings his firstborn into the world, he says, 'Let all God's angels worship him'"* (Hebrews 1:6).
- By doing His word concerning His commandments.
- By heeding the voice of His word as proclaimed by the saints on earth.
- By caring for those who will receive salvation: *"Then he lay down under the tree and fell asleep. All at once an angel touched him and said, 'Get up and eat'"* (1 Kings 19:5).
- Ministering spirits: *"Are not all angels ministering spirits sent to serve those who will inherit salvation?"* (Heb. 1:14). *"The time came when the beggar died and the angels carried him to Abraham's side..."* (Luke 16:22).

Angels Minister Divine Strength

Angels ministered to Jesus in the Garden of Gethsemane and after His forty-day fast.

Then I fainted lying face downward on the ground. But he roused me with a touch, and helped me to my feet (Daniel 8:18 TLB).

Then the devil left Him, and angels came and attended Him (Matthew 4:11).

Angels Are Involved in Healing

For an angel went down at a certain time into the pool and stirred up the water; then whoever stepped in first, after the stirring of the water, was made well of whatever disease he had (John 5:4 NKJV).

Angels Provide Guidance

See, I am sending an angel ahead of you to guard you along the way and to bring you to the place I have prepared. Pay attention to him and listen to what he says. Do not rebel against him; he will not forgive your rebellion, since my Name is in him. If you listen carefully to what he says and do all that I say, I will be an enemy to your enemies and will oppose those who oppose you. My angel will go ahead of you and bring you into the land of the Amorites, Hittites, Perizzites, Canaanites, Hivites and Jebusites, and I will wipe them out (Exodus 23:20-23).

We must pay more careful attention, therefore, to what we have heard, so that we do not drift away. For if the message spoken by angels was binding, and every violation and disobedience received its just punishment, how shall we escape if we ignore such a great salvation? This salvation, which was first announced by the Lord, was confirmed to us by those who heard Him (Hebrews 2:1-3).

Angels Guide Sinners to the Gospel

Angels direct people to where the Gospel is being preached. For example, an angel told Cornelius to send for Peter so that the Gospel could come to the Gentiles. See Acts 10:1-6.

An angel told Philip to go to the desert to minister to the Ethiopians.

Now an angel of the Lord said to Philip, "Go south to the road—the desert road—that goes down from Jerusalem to Gaza." So he started out, and on his way he met an Ethiopian eunuch, an important official in charge of all the treasury of Candace, queen of the Ethiopians. This man had gone to Jerusalem to worship (Acts 8:26-27).

Philip's encounter with the Ethiopian man in Acts 8 was actually the fulfillment of a prophetic word given by David: *"Princes shall come out of Egypt; Ethiopia shall soon stretch out her hands unto God"* (Ps. 68:31 KJV). The angel guided Philip to fulfill a prophetic utterance spoken long before then. He ministered to this Ethiopian man who returned and spread the Gospel to his nation.

Angels Camp Around the Saints

The angel of the Lord encamps around those who fear Him, and He delivers them (Psalm 34:7).

When the servant of the man of God got up and went out early the next morning, an army with horses and chariots had surrounded the city. "Oh, my lord, what shall we do?" the servant asked. "Don't be afraid," the prophet answered. "Those who are with us are more than those who are with them." And Elisha prayed, "O Lord, open his eyes so that he may see." Then the Lord opened the servant's eyes, and he looked and saw the hills full of horses and chariots of fire all around Elisha (2 Kings 6:15-17).

Angels Rescue the Saints

If you make the Most High your dwelling—even the Lord, who is my refuge—then no harm will befall you, no disaster will come near your tent. For He will command His angels concerning you to guard you in all your ways; they will lift you up in their hands, so that you will not strike your foot against a stone (Psalm 91:9-12).

Then the high priest and all his associates, who were members of the party of the Sadducees, were filled with jealousy. They arrested the apostles and put them in the public jail. But during the night an angel of the Lord opened the doors of the jail and brought them out. "Go, stand in the temple courts," he said, "and tell the people the full message of this new life" (Acts 5:17-20).

Angels Are Instruments of God's Judgment

May they be like chaff before the wind, with the angel of the Lord driving them away; may their path be dark and slippery, with the angel of the Lord pursuing them (Psalm 35:5-6).

Then I heard a loud voice from the temple saying to the seven angels, "Go, pour out the seven bowls of God's wrath on the earth" (Revelation 16:1).

So the Lord sent a plague on Israel from that morning until the end of the time designated, and seventy thousand of the people from Dan to Beersheba died. When the angel stretched out his hand to destroy Jerusalem, the Lord was grieved because of the calamity and said to the angel who was afflicting the people, "Enough! Withdraw your hand." The angel of the Lord was then at the threshing floor of Araunah the Jebusite (2 Samuel 24:15-16).

Angels Celebrate the Praises of God

Then I looked and heard the voice of many angels, numbering thousands upon thousands, and ten thousand times ten thousand. They encircled the throne and the living creatures and the elders. In a loud voice they sang: 'Worthy is the Lamb, who was slain, to receive power and wealth and wisdom and strength and honor and glory and praise! (Revelation 5:11-12)

Who laid its cornerstone—while the morning stars sang together and all the angels shouted for joy (Job 38:6b-7).

Praise Him, all His angels; praise Him, all his heavenly hosts (Psalm 148:2).

The Law Was Given by the Mediation of the Angels

For if the message spoken by angels was binding, and every violation and disobedience received its just punishment, how shall we escape if we ignore such a great salvation? This salvation, which was first announced by the Lord, was confirmed to us by those who heard Him (Hebrews 2:2-3).

Was there ever a prophet your fathers did not persecute? They even killed those who predicted the coming of the Righteous One. And now you have betrayed and murdered him—you who have received the law that was put into effect through angels but have not obeyed it (Acts 7:52-53).

Angels Carry Out the Purposes of God

But God was very angry when he went, and the angel of the Lord stood in the road to oppose him. Balaam was riding on his donkey, and his two servants were with him (Numbers 22:22).

Angels Do the Will of God

He answered, "The one who sowed the good seed is the Son of Man. The field is the world, and the good seed stands for the sons of the kingdom. The weeds are the sons of the evil one, and the enemy who sows them is the devil. The harvest is the end of the age, and the harvesters are angels. As the weeds are pulled up and burned in the fire, so it will be at the end of the age. The Son of Man will send out His angels, and they will weed out of His kingdom everything that causes sin and all who do evil. They will throw them into the fiery furnace, where there will be weeping and gnashing of teeth (Matthew 13:37-42).

Angels Bring Blessings From God

For an angel went down at a certain time into the pool and stirred up the water; then whoever stepped in first, after the stirring of the water, was made well of whatever disease he had (John 5:4 NKJV).

Angels Are Involved in Advancing the Church

Angels assist in advancing the Church through angelic carriage of messages. The Book of Acts reveals angelic intervention on behalf of Cornelius, and the Church was enlarged to include the Gentiles. See Acts 10:1-6.

Angels Will Accompany the Lord in the Second Coming

The Lord Himself will descend with the voice of an archangel:

Brothers, we do not want you to be ignorant about those who fall asleep, or to grieve like the rest of men, who have no hope. We believe that Jesus died and rose again and so we believe that God will bring with Jesus those who have fallen asleep in Him. According to the Lord's own word, we tell you that we who are still alive, who are left till the coming of the Lord, will certainly not precede those who have fallen asleep. For the Lord Himself will come down from heaven, with a loud command, with the voice of the archangel and with the trumpet call of God, and the dead in Christ will rise first. After that, we who are still alive and are left will be caught up together with them in the clouds to meet the Lord in the air. And so we will be with the Lord forever. Therefore encourage each other with these words (1 Thessalonians 4:13-18).

Angels Will Fight in the Final Battle With Satan

When the thousand years are over, satan will be released from his prison and will go out to deceive the nations in the four corners of the earth—Gog and Magog—to gather them for battle. In number they are like the sand on the seashore. They marched across the breadth of the earth and surrounded the camp of God's people, the city he loves. But fire came down from heaven and devoured them (Revelation 20:7-9).

THE CATEGORIES OF ANGELS

There is not enough information in the Scriptures to fully categorize the angelic realm, but from what does exist, angels can be placed into the following ranks.

The Angel of the Lord

There is a high probability that the Angel of the Lord involves the pre-incarnate appearances of Jesus Christ, the Son of God. Many times the Angel of the Lord was used to indicate the manifestation of God Himself. The Angel of the Lord is an uncreated angel distinguished from other angels and identified in many instances in the Scriptures as the Lord God, as we will see in this chapter. This Angel appears as the Lord God of the Old Testament and as Jesus Christ in the New Testament.

The Angel of the Lord's deity is clearly portrayed in the Bible; for instance, this Angel received worship from Joshua and was often used interchangeably in the Scriptures with the Lord and God. Compare how the terms are used in Acts 7:30-34 and Exodus 3:2-6 though both passages speak of the same event.

> *And when forty years had passed, an Angel of the Lord appeared to him in a flame of fire in a bush, in the wilderness of Mount Sinai. When Moses saw it, he marveled at the sight; and as he drew near to observe, the voice of the Lord came to him, saying, "I am the God of your fathers—the God of Abraham, the God of Isaac, and the God of Jacob." And Moses trembled and dared not look. Then the Lord said to him, "Take your sandals off your feet, for the place where you stand is holy ground. I have surely seen the oppression of My people who are in Egypt; I have heard their groaning and have come down to deliver them. And now come, I will send you to Egypt" (Acts 7:30-34 NKJV).*

> *There the angel of the Lord appeared to him in flames of fire from within a bush. Moses saw that though the bush was on fire it did not burn up. So Moses thought, "I will go over and see this strange sight —why the bush does not burn up." When the Lord saw that he had gone over to look, God called to him from within the bush, "Moses! Moses!" And Moses said, "Here I am." "Do not come any closer," God said. "Take off your sandals, for the place where you are standing is holy ground." Then he said, "I am the God of your father, the God of Abraham, the God of Isaac and the God of Jacob." At this, Moses hid his face, because he was afraid to look at God (Exodus 3:2-6).*

The Cambridge Bible comment about this passage: There is a fascinating forecast of the coming Messiah, breaking through the dimness with amazing consistency, at intervals from Genesis to Malachi; Abraham, Moses, the slave girl Hagar, the impoverished farmer Gideon, even the humble parents of Samson, had seen and talked with Him centuries before the herald angels proclaimed His (Jesus Christ) birth in Bethlehem.

Also He did not appear again after Christ came in human form, died, and ascended into heaven.

The Archangel

An archangel reveals or manifests God's authority, dominion, and rule in the heavenlies in the service of God. Only one archangel was mentioned in the Scriptures, but it is believed that angel Gabriel is also in this category and also lucifer who became satan.

Michael is one of chief princes, a high-ranking warrior and the only one named as an archangel in Scriptures. Michael contested for the body of Moses, fought and defeated satan and his angel in heaven. All of the places he was mentioned in the Bible were in connection with spiritual warfare.

> *In the very same way, these dreamers pollute their own bodies, reject authority and slander celestial beings. But even the archangel Michael, when he was disputing with the devil about the body of Moses, did not dare to bring a slanderous accusation against him, but said, "The Lord rebuke you!" (Jude 8-9)*

> *But the prince of the Persian kingdom resisted me twenty-one days. Then Michael, one of the chief princes, came to help me, because I was detained there with the king of Persia. Now I have come to explain to you what will happen to your people in the future, for the vision concerns a time yet to come (Daniel 10:13-14).*

> *And there was war in heaven. Michael and his angels fought against the dragon, and the dragon and his angels fought back. But he was not strong enough, and they lost their place in heaven. The great dragon was hurled down—that ancient serpent called the devil, or Satan,*

who leads the whole world astray. He was hurled to the earth, and his angels with him (Revelation 12:7-9).

According to the Lord's own word, we tell you that we who are still alive, who are left till the coming of the Lord, will certainly not precede those who have fallen asleep. For the Lord Himself will come down from heaven, with a loud command, with the voice of the archangel and with the trumpet call of God, and the dead in Christ will rise first. After that, we who are still alive and are left will be caught up together with them in the clouds to meet the Lord in the air. And so we will be with the Lord forever. Therefore encourage each other with these words (1 Thessalonians 4:15-18).

The Bible also describes the role of archangel Michael in the end times.

At that time Michael, the great prince who protects your people, will arise. There will be a time of distress such as has not happened from the beginning of nations until then. But at that time your people—everyone whose name is found written in the book—will be delivered. Multitudes who sleep in the dust of the earth will awake: some to everlasting life, others to shame and everlasting contempt. Those who are wise will shine like the brightness of the heavens, and those who lead many to righteousness, like the stars for ever and ever. But you, Daniel, close up and seal the words of the scroll until the time of the end. Many will go here and there to increase knowledge (Daniel 12:1-4).

Gabriel is the messenger/knowledge angel. He describes himself as the one who stands in the presence of God. This angel brought almost all of the major news items to humanity from Heaven.

While I, Daniel, was watching the vision and trying to understand it, there before me stood one who looked like a man. And I heard a man's voice from the Ulai calling, "Gabriel, tell this man the meaning of the vision." As he came near the place where I was standing, I was terrified and fell prostrate. "Son of man," he said to me, "understand that the vision concerns the time of the end" (Daniel 8:15-17).

While I was speaking and praying, confessing my sin and the sin of my people Israel and making my request to the Lord my God for His holy hill—while I was still in prayer, Gabriel, the man I had seen in the earlier vision, came to me in swift flight about the time of the evening sacrifice. He instructed me and said to me, "Daniel, I have now come to give you insight and understanding. As soon as you began to pray, an answer was given, which I have come to tell you, for you are highly esteemed. Therefore, consider the message and understand the vision" (Daniel 9:20-23).

The angel answered, "I am Gabriel. I stand in the presence of God, and I have been sent to speak to you and to tell you this good news" (Luke 1:19).

Guardian Angels

Guardian angels watch over us. Each one of us has our own private guardian angels. Evangelist Billy Graham, observing the plural in the terms in Psalm 91:11-12, *"For He will command His angels concerning you to guard you in all your ways; they will lift you up in their hands, so that you will not strike your foot against a stone,"* concluded that each believer must have at least two angels whose assigned duty is to protect the person. Guardian angels keep us from falling, getting lost, or stumbling into unknown dangers in the unseen realm of the spirits.

Jesus said, *"See that you do not look down on one of these little ones* [childlike believers or those with the humbling of a child expressed in humble service]. *For I tell you that their angels in heaven always see the face of my Father in heaven* (Matt. 18:10).

Guardian angels are the angels of innocence. In our spiritual simplicity, our guardian angels are much activated. We see a guardian angel helping Philip in Acts

8:26: *"Now an angel of the Lord said to Philip, 'Go south to the road—the desert road—that goes down from Jerusalem to Gaza."*

THE ORDER OF ANGELS

The Order of Cherubim

Cherubim is mentioned 91 times in the Bible. A cherubim is an angelic creature of high rank first mentioned in the Scriptures after God drove Adam and Eve out of Eden. Cherubs were posted at the entrance of the Garden with flaming swords to guard the tree of life. They are covering angels associated with worshiping God. God asked Moses to put two cherubim to cover the mercy seats in Tabernacle. Lucifer was described as the anointed guardian cherub in the Book of Ezekiel, so satan is of this ancestry.

Cherubim often act as the chariot upon which the throne of God rides: *"He also gave him the plan for the chariot, that is, the cherubim of gold that spread their wings and shelter the ark of the covenant of the Lord"* (1 Chron. 28:18). The Bible describes the throne of God in motion in Ezekiel 1. David spoke of God riding on the cherub: *"He mounted the cherubim and flew; He soared on the wings of the wind"* (2 Sam. 22:11). *"He mounted the cherubim and flew; He soared on the wings of the wind"* (Ps. 18:10).

Cherubim are also the angels that cover:

> *The priests then brought the ark of the Lord's covenant to its place in the inner sanctuary of the temple, the Most Holy Place, and put it beneath the wings of the cherubim. The cherubim spread their wings over the place of the ark and overshadowed the ark and its carrying poles* (1 Kings 8:6-7).

> *Behind the second curtain was a room called the Most Holy Place, which had the golden altar of incense and the gold-covered ark of the covenant. This ark contained the gold jar of manna, Aaron's staff that had budded, and the stone tablets of the covenant. Above the ark were*

the cherubim of the Glory, overshadowing the atonement cover. But we cannot discuss these things in detail now (Hebrews 9:3-5).

Make an atonement cover of pure gold—two and a half cubits long and a cubit and a half wide. And make two cherubim out of hammered gold at the ends of the cover. Make one cherub on one end and the second cherub on the other; make the cherubim of one piece with the cover, at the two ends. The cherubim are to have their wings spread upwards, overshadowing the cover with them. The cherubim are to face each other, looking toward the cover. Place the cover on top of the ark and put in the ark the Testimony, which I will give you (Exodus 25:17-21).

The cherubim's main function in the throne room is that of covering and swift transportation.

The Order of Seraphim

Seraphim are stationed above the Throne Room. *Seraphim* means "the burning ones." They rank very high among the angels in privileges and honor. *Seraph,* meaning the "burning or fiery ones," are angelic creatures stationed about the throne of God in Heaven. They minister to God with humility and majesty. The ministry of seraphim is closely associated with promises and glory of God. They are burning or fiery in appearance and motions. Seraphim are seen demonstrating humility and modesty as they praise God with their faces always covered with their hands (see Isaiah 6:1-4).

Living Creatures

Living creatures are high celestial beings, angels of watchfulness and revelation. They are creations covered with eyes all around, even under their wings; they appear to be proclaimers of God's holiness and eternal nature. In Ezekiel 10, *the prophet Ezekiel describes the living creatures as cherubim.* The living creatures transport the throne of God. In Ezekiel chapters 1 and 10, the prophet Ezekiel saw the throne of

God in motion being carried by the living creatures. They are also creatures of the highest level of revelations (see Ezekiel 10:13-17).

> *I looked, and I saw a windstorm coming out of the north—an immense cloud with flashing lightning and surrounded by brilliant light. The center of the fire looked like glowing metal, and in the fire was what looked like four living creatures. In appearance their form was that of a man, but each of them had four faces and four wings. Their legs were straight; their feet were like those of a calf and gleamed like burnished bronze. Under their wings on their four sides they had the hands of a man. All four of them had faces and wings, and their wings touched one another. Each one went straight ahead; they did not turn as they moved. Their faces looked like this: Each of the four had the face of a man, and on the right side each had the face of a lion, and on the left the face of an ox; each also had the face of an eagle* (Ezekiel 1:4-10).

> *Also before the throne there was what looked like a sea of glass, clear as crystal. In the center, around the throne, were four living creatures, and they were covered with eyes, in front and back. The first living creature was like a lion, the second was like an ox, the third had a face like a man, the fourth was like a flying eagle. Each of the four living creatures had six wings and was covered with eyes all around, even under his wings. Day and night they never stop saying: "Holy, holy, holy is the Lord God Almighty, who was, and is, and is to come"* (Revelation 4:6-8).

FOUR ASPECTS OF THE NATURE OF GOD

The four faces of these creatures, as seen through the eyes of Ezekiel and apostle John, portray aspects of the character of God. Their likeness to the form of earthly creatures being only representative of the aspects of God's character that is symbolized.

Symbol Reflected by the Four Faces	Aspects of God Probably Portrayed
Face of a lion	*Majesty, power or strength, supremacy, and courage*
Face of a ox	*Faithfulness, perseverance, patience, and servanthood*
Face of a man	*Intelligence, royalty (nobility), and wisdom*
Face of an eagle	*Sovereignty or divinity, devotion, deity, and divine mystery*

Common Angels

Common angels are those who appear to the saints and minister to the heirs of salvation.

DECLARATIONS

"Thou shalt also decree a thing, and it shall be established unto thee..." (Job 22:28 KJV).

1. God help me to be loyal to You and be faithful to Your covenant and so grant me the favor of confiding in me and reveal Your secrets to me.

    "The Lord confides in those who fear Him; He makes His covenant known to them" (Psalm 25:14).

2. I shall live by faith in God for I now consider everything nothing for the sake of Christ my Lord.

    "But my righteous one will live by faith. And if he shrinks back, I will not be pleased with him. But we are not of those who shrink back and are destroyed, but of those who believe and are saved" (Hebrews 10:38-39).

    "But whatever was to my profit I now consider loss for the sake of Christ. What is more, I consider everything a loss compared to the surpassing greatness of knowing Christ Jesus my Lord, for whose sake I have lost all things. I consider them rubbish, that I may gain Christ and be found in Him, not having a righteousness of my own that comes from the law, but that which is through faith in Christ—the righteousness that comes from God and is by faith. I want to know Christ and the power of His resurrection and the fellowship of sharing in His sufferings, becoming like Him in His death, and so, somehow, to attain to the resurrection from the dead. Not that I have already obtained all this, or have already been made perfect, but I press on to take hold of that for which Christ Jesus took hold of me. Brothers, I do not consider myself yet to have taken hold of it. But one thing I do: Forgetting what is behind and straining toward what is ahead, I press on toward the goal to win the prize for which God has called me heavenward in Christ Jesus" (Philippians 3:7-14).

Chapter 15

HOW TO
ENGAGE ANGELS

THE BIBLE GIVES CLEAR rules on what the angels are, what they do, how they do what they do, how we are to relate to them, and at whose commands they are moved. God created angels as the Bible says, *"Who maketh His angels spirits; His ministers a flaming fire"* (Ps. 104:4 KJV).

In the present dispensation, angels revolve around the establishment of the Church of Jesus Christ and in advancing and building up the Body of Christ.

> *"See, I am sending an angel ahead of you to guard you along the way and to bring you to the place I have prepared. Pay attention to him and listen to what he says. Do not rebel against him; he will not forgive your rebellion, since My name is in him"* (Exodus 23:20-21).

From this passage in Exodus 23, we can see that angels can be instructed by God to guard the saints when necessary. Also they can help the saints achieve their God-given purpose and destiny in life. Angels are representatives of God with specific missions and are against anything or anyone who hinders their fulfillment of their assignment: *"Pay attention to him and listen to what he says. Do not rebel against him; he will not forgive your rebellion, since My name is in him."*

CHANNEL OF COMMUNICATION WITH ANGELS

Even though angels are by and large superhuman in power, they are empowered by the prayers of the saints in an indirect way. Prayers to God cause God to release the angels, so it is God who has the sovereign control of the release and angelic assignment. This channel keeps people from worshiping angels. Angels are thereafter activated by God's Word once on assignment. Man limits the power of angels when he speaks negative words, complains, and speaks unbelieving words instead of speaking God's Word. Apostle Peter says in Acts 12:11, *"Then Peter came to himself and said, 'Now I know without a doubt **that the Lord sent His angel and rescued me from Herod's clutches and from everything the Jewish people were anticipating.'"***

Angels do not do man's bidding. Man does not have the power to release angels and does not command angels.

> *Bless the Lord, ye His angels, that excel in strength, that do His commandments, hearkening unto the voice of His word* (Psalm 103:20 KJV).

**Prayers to God cause God to release the angels, so it is
God who has the sovereign control of the
release and angelic assignment.**

Angels heed the voice of the Word of God. It is pertinent to know that angels are not sentimental, as they are heavenly assistants sent forth under strict instruction to carry out assignments as angels on assignment. They could be on assignment independent of human action, but most times they are on conditional assignments, the eventual outcome of which depends on human actions or reactions. God respects the human right of choice.

Jesus said, *"Or do you think that I cannot now pray to My Father, and He will provide Me with more than twelve legions of angels?"* (Matt. 26:53 NKJV). We do not command the release of angels, we pray to God to release angels. When you pray and ask God for help, He dispatches angels to deliver you from the enemy. As we see in Psalm 35:5, *"Let them be as chaff before the wind, and let the angel of the Lord chase them."* A tremendous New Testament example of this is found in the story of the apostle Peter who was delivered from prison by an angel (see Acts 12).

How Manoah interacted with the Angel of the Lord teaches us a few lessons on how to relate and work with angels:

> *The angel of the Lord appeared to her and said, "You are sterile and childless, but you are going to conceive and have a son. Now see to it that you drink no wine or other fermented drink and that you do not eat anything unclean, because you will conceive and give birth to a son. No razor may be used on his head, because the boy is to be a Nazir- ite, set apart to God from birth, and he will begin the deliverance of Israel from the hands of the Philistines." Then the woman went to her husband and told him, "A man of God came to me. He looked like an angel of God, very awesome. I didn't ask him where he came from, and he didn't tell me his name. But he said to me, 'You will conceive and give birth to a son. Now then, drink no wine or other fermented drink and do not eat anything unclean, because the boy will be a Nazirite of God from birth until the day of his death.' "Then Manoah prayed to the Lord: "O Lord, I beg you, let the man of God you sent to us come again to teach us how to bring up the boy who is to be born." God heard Manoah, and the angel of God came again to the woman while she was out in the field; but her husband Manoah was not with her. The woman hurried to tell her husband, "He's here! The man who appeared to me the other day!" Manoah got up and followed his wife. When he came to the man, he said, "Are you the one who talked to my wife?" "I am," he said. So Manoah asked him, "When your words are fulfilled, what is to be the rule for the boy's life and work?" The angel of the Lord answered, "Your wife must do all that I have told her. She must not eat anything that comes from the grapevine, nor drink any wine or other fermented drink nor eat anything unclean. She must do everything I have commanded her." Manoah said to the angel of*

the Lord, "We would like you to stay until we prepare a young goat for you." The angel of the Lord replied, "Even though you detain me, I will not eat any of your food. But if you prepare a burnt offering, offer it to the Lord." (Manoah did not realize that it was the angel of the Lord.) Then Manoah inquired of the angel of the Lord, "What is your name, so that we may honor you when your word comes true?" He replied, "Why do you ask my name? It is beyond understanding. "Then Manoah took a young goat, together with the grain offering, and sacrificed it on a rock to the Lord. And the Lord did an amazing thing while Manoah and his wife watched: As the flame blazed up from the altar toward heaven, the angel of the Lord ascended in the flame. Seeing this, Manoah and his wife fell with their faces to the ground (Judges 13:3-20).

Angels do not do man's bidding. Man does not have the power to release angels and does not command angels.

When relating to angels, remember:

- Ask God to release them through prayers.
- Use the Word of God because angels harken to the voice of God's Word.
- Angels work in the name of the Lord.
- Angels can give us guidance from God.
- Angels can bring promises of God to us on earth.
- We do not worship angels nor build memorials for them.
- We should speak the will of God when relating to angels.
- We should speak the word of faith when relating to angels.
- Maintain a right standing with God.
- Be sensitive in the spirit to know the "now" will of God on the issue.

- That angels are not only encamping around us, they are also listening to what we say.

We know that ***angels are indirectly empowered by the prayers of the saints*** by reading Daniel 10:7-14 and in the following passage:

> *So Peter was kept in prison, but the church was earnestly praying to God for him. The night before Herod was to bring him to trial, Peter was sleeping between two soldiers, bound with two chains, and sentries stood guard at the entrance. Suddenly an angel of the Lord appeared and a light shone in the cell. He struck Peter on the side and woke him up. "Quick, get up!" he said, and the chains fell off Peter's wrists. Then the angel said to him, "Put on your clothes and sandals." And Peter did so. "Wrap your cloak around you and follow me," the angel told him. Peter followed him out of the prison, but he had no idea that what the angel was doing was really happening; he thought he was seeing a vision. They passed the first and second guards and came to the Iron Gate leading to the city. It opened for them by itself, and they went through it. When they had walked the length of one street, suddenly the angel left him. Then Peter came to himself and said, "Now I know without a doubt that the Lord sent his angel and rescued me from Herod's clutches and from everything the Jewish people were anticipating"* (Acts 12:5-11).

Angels heed the voice of the Word of God.

The Church prayed to God and the angel was released. Daniel prayed and humbled himself, it was heard in Heaven and an angel was released.

> *Then another angel, having a golden censer, came and stood at the altar. He was given much incense, that he should offer it with the prayers of all the saints upon the golden altar which was before the throne. And*

the smoke of the incense, with the prayers of the saints, ascended before God from the angel's hand (Revelation 8:3-4 NKJV).

DISOBEDIENCE PROVOKES ANGELS

With the coming of dawn, the angels urged Lot, saying, "Hurry! Take your wife and your two daughters who are here, or you will be swept away when the city is punished." When he hesitated, the men grasped his hand and the hands of his wife and of his two daughters and led them safely out of the city, for the Lord was merciful to them. As soon as they had brought them out, one of them said, "Flee for your lives! Don't look back, and don't stop anywhere in the plain! Flee to the mountains or you will be swept away!" (Genesis 19:15-17)

But the day Lot left Sodom, fire and sulphur rained down from heaven and destroyed them all. It will be just like this on the day the Son of Man is revealed. On that day no-one who is on the roof of his house, with his goods inside, should go down to get them. Likewise, no-one in the field should go back for anything. Remember Lot's wife! (Luke 17:29-32)

Angels are provoked when the Word of God or His promises are not mixed with faith (see Exodus 23:20-21), and when we resist them in their assignment from God (see Luke 1:11-15).

Angels are also provoked when negative words or words contrary to the Word or will of God are spoken (see Ecclesiastes 5:1-2 and 5:6). Doubts or unbelief will bind your angels.

DECLARATIONS

"Thou shalt also decree a thing, and it shall be established unto thee..."
(Job 22:28 KJV).

1. God will help us unite in plans and purposes that our prayers shall avail much.

   "Again, I tell you that if two of you on earth agree about anything you ask for, it will be done for you by My Father in heaven" (Matthew 18:19).

2. The life I now live I live in Christ Jesus, there can no longer be any condemnation since I am in Christ.

   "I have been crucified with Christ and I no longer live, but Christ lives in me. The life I live in the body, I live by faith in the Son of God, who loved me and gave Himself for me" (Galatians 2:20).

3. God, help me to keep my focus on You and let the mind of Christ be the mind that I have.

   "Since, then, you have been raised with Christ, set your hearts on things above, where Christ is seated at the right hand of God. Set your minds on things above, not on earthly things. For you died, and your life is now hidden with Christ in God. When Christ, who is your life, appears, then you also will appear with Him in glory" (Colossians 3:1-4).

Conclusion

THE ULTIMATE JUSTICE

TOTAL REDEMPTION OF HUMANKIND AND CREATION

THE JUSTICE OF GOD is much more than judgment and punishment, it is the totality of all that God has put in place to ensure everything happens and everyone gets the fairness that can only be given by and received from Him. The ultimate justice is the total redemption of the fallen man and the fallen creation.

On a corporate level, there are the ever-increasing blatant displays of moral decadence, sexual profanity, and, as predicted, *"the love of many"* has grown cold; yet I have the audacity to continue to believe that God has all things on hand and He holds the firmaments of the heavens and the earth.

> *For by Him all things were created that are in heaven and on earth, visible and invisible, whether **thrones** or **dominions** or **principalities** or **powers**. All things were created through Him and for Him* (Colossians 1:16).

God wants all people to realize that human intellect is limited and cannot completely fathom the depth and breadth of the nature of His justice. The Bible says, *"Who will bring any charge against those whom God has chosen?* ***It is God who*** *justifies"* (Rom. 8:33). Every now and again, we face challenges that bear credence to the fact that God alone can justify a person. It is the realization that every flesh will fail that drives us to the One, the Eternal God, who never fails.

It is my wish that you know that God is uniquely powerful as He is uniquely just. True to this nature, He allows a divine system that ensures His justice. The geographical jurisdiction of this divine justice has no restriction; it applies anywhere and at any time. After the Second World War, the Allied Forces faced a moral and judicial dilemma. They did not know what to do with the evil perpetuators of the horrendous crimes of that war. Under which laws were they to try the Nazis? But with God this is not so. God's justice has no such limitations. It applies everywhere and to everyone, whether Jew or Gentile, slave or free, king or subjects, rich or poor, young or old, male or female. His justice is no respecter of persons. Above all, His justice has universal standards of right or wrong and a code of conduct that none can escape.

Consciously or unconsciously, our trust in God is interwoven with our belief in His justice. Somehow this confidence stems from the dependability and reliability of God, which never fail. Hidden within every person is the belief that the justice of God will one day bring vengeance on any injustice. Perhaps, that is why Job was able to say, *"I know that my Redeemer lives, and that in the end He will stand upon the earth"* (Job 19:25) in spite of all that came across his path in life.

Spiritual principles work for everyone. According to the law of justice of God, if you do not obey God, no matter who you are, you will suffer the bitter consequences.

> *If you will only let Me help you, if you will only obey, then I will make you rich! But if you keep on turning your backs and refusing to listen to Me, you will be killed by your enemies; I, the Lord, have spoken* (Isaiah 1:19-20 TLB).

If you are willing and obedient, you will eat the best of the land.

> *"Come now, let us reason together," says the Lord. "Though your sins are like scarlet, they shall be as white as snow; though they are red as*

crimson, they shall be like wool. **If you are willing and obedient, you will eat the best from the land** (Isaiah 1:18-19).

And again He warned, *"You don't believe me? If you want me to protect you,* **you must learn to believe** *what I say"* (Isa. 7:9b TLB).

I have not written about all of the things that God does to bring supreme justice to the earth, but I have shared many things about the justice of God. I hope you have learned about His unfailing love and grace, how to connect with the heavenly realms, how to access His blessings for you, and how to work with His angels.

And finally, God said of Jesus Christ that He would bring justice to the nations: *"Here is my Servant, whom I uplifted, My chosen One in whom I delight, I will put My Spirit in Him and He will* **bring justice to the nations"** (Isa. 42:1).

The Bible declares, **"Righteousness and justice** *are the foundation of Your throne; love and faithfulness go before You"* (Psalm 89:14).

> *For I, the Lord, love justice; I hate robbery and iniquity. In my faithfulness I will reward them and make an everlasting covenant with them* (Isaiah 61:8).

Here is the final conclusion of all that has been written:

> *Now all has been heard; here is the conclusion of the matter: Fear God and keep His commandment, for this is the whole duty of man. For God will bring every deed into judgment, including every hidden thing, whether it is good or evil* (Ecclesiastes 12:13-14).

In the Gospel of Matthew, the Bible says Christ will lead justice to victory:

> *Here is my servant whom I have chosen, the One I love, in whom I delight; I will put My Spirit on Him, and He will proclaim justice to the nations. He will not quarrel or cry out; no one will hear His voice in the streets. A bruised reed He will not break, and a smouldering wick He will not snuff out, till He leads justice to victory. In His name the nations will put their hope"* (Matthew 12:18-21).

LEADING JUSTICE TO VICTORY

God is committed to reclaiming this fallen world and rescuing sinful people through His Son Jesus Christ, *"to be put into effect when the times will have reached their fulfillment—to bring all things in heaven and on earth together under one head, even Christ"* (Eph. 1:10).

In manner reminiscent of Noah's story, God promises a new earth and a new heaven: *"Behold, I will create new heavens and a new earth. The former things will not be remembered, nor will they come to mind"* (Isa. 65:17).

Unfortunately, like in Noah's generation, not everyone will make it to the new earth and the new heaven. Just like the story of Noah was a message of hope in the wicked generation that Noah lived in, so the Bible says, *"...to him who overcomes, I will give the right to eat from the tree of life, which is in the paradise of God"* (Rev. 2:7). And also, *"to him who overcomes and does my will to the end, I will give authority over the nations"* (Rev. 2:26). The writer of the Book of Hebrew reiterated this saying, *"But we are not of those who shrink back and are destroyed, but of those who believe and are saved"* (Heb. 10:39). I am assured that the righteous shall not perish with the ungodly.

On our part, we have to repent and turn toward God. *"Repent, then, and turn to God, so that your sins may be wiped out, that times of refreshing may come from the Lord, **and that He may send the Christ, who has been appointed for you—even Jesus. He must remain in heaven until the time comes for God to restore everything, as He promised long ago through His holy prophets"*** (Acts 3:19-21).

Apostle Peter admonished us to take ***today*** and each day seriously, for the day of reckoning will come without notice upon humanity: *"But the day of the Lord will come like a thief. The heavens will disappear with a roar; the elements will be destroyed by fire, and the earth and everything in it will be laid bare. Since everything will be destroyed in this way, what kind of people ought you to be? You ought to live holy and godly lives as you look forward to the day of God and speed its coming. That day will bring about the destruction of the heavens by fire, and the elements will melt in the heat. But in keeping with His promise we are **looking forward to a new heaven and a new earth, the home of righteousness.** So then, dear friends, since you are looking* *forward to this, make every effort to be found spotless, blameless and at peace with Him"* (2 Pet. 3:10-14).

Ultimately, God will redeem the righteous as the apostle John says, *"Then I saw **a new heaven and a new earth**, for the first heaven and the first earth had passed away, and there was no longer any sea. I saw the Holy City, the New Jerusalem, coming down out of heaven from God, prepared as a bride beautifully dressed for her husband"* (Rev. 21:1-2).

The final justice is not only to regain a perfect earth, but also a perfect peace and harmony and much more. By word of knowledge revelation, the prophet Isaiah described harmony of the future home of Christians, a world of harmony between humankind and all animals and between animal and animal; once again the Garden of Eden will be regained and even much more:

> *The wolf will live with the lamb, the leopard will lie down with the goat, the calf and the lion and the yearling together; and a little child will lead them. The cow will feed with the bear, their young will lie down together, and the lion will eat straw like the ox. The infant will play near the hole of the cobra, and the young child put his hand into the viper's nest. They will neither harm nor destroy on all My holy mountain, for the earth will be full of the knowledge of the Lord as the waters cover the sea (Isaiah 11:6-9).*

This is the ultimate justice of God.

ABOUT THE AUTHOR

DR. JOE IBOJIE, founder and senior pastor of The Father's House, travels nationally and internationally as a Bible and prophetic teacher. He combines a unique prophetic gifting with rare insight into the mysteries of God and the ancient biblical methods of understanding dreams and visions. His ministry has blessed thousands by bringing down-to-earth clarity to the prophetic ministry. He is a popular speaker worldwide. He and his wife, Cynthia, live in Aberdeen, Scotland.

CONTACT INFORMATION

For additional copies of this book and other products from Cross House Books,
Contact: sales@crosshousebooks.co.uk.
Please visit our Website for product updates and news at
www.crosshousebooks.co.uk.

OTHER INQUIRIES

CROSS HOUSE BOOKS
Christian Book Publishers
245 Midstocket Road
Aberdeen, AB15 5PH, UK
info@crosshousebooks.co.uk
publisher@crosshousebooks.co.uk
"The entrance of Your Word brings light."

MINISTRY INFORMATION

DR. JOE IBOJIE IS THE SENIOR PASTOR OF
THE FATHER'S HOUSE

A family church and a vibrant community of Christians located in Aberdeen
Scotland, UK. The Father's House seeks to build a bridge of hope across generations, racial divides, and gender biases through the ministry of the Word.

You are invited to come and worship if you are in the area.

For location, please visit the church's Website:

www.the-fathers-house.org.uk

For inquiries:

info@the-fathers-house.org.uk

Call 44 1224 701343

How to Live the Supernatural Life in the Here and Now

Are you ready to stop living an ordinary life? You were meant to live a supernatural life! God intends us to experience His power every day! In *How to Live the Supernatural Life in the Here and Now* you will learn how to bring the supernatural power of God into everyday living. Finding the proper balance for your life allows you to step into the supernatural and to move in power and authority over everything around you. Dr. Joe Ibojie, an experienced pastor and prolific writer, provides practical steps and instruction that will help you to:

- Step out of the things that hold you back in life.
- Understand that all life is spiritual.
- Experience the supernatural life that God has planned for you!
- Find balance between the natural and the spiritual.
- Release God's power to change and empower your circumstances.

Are you ready to live a life of spiritual harmony? Then you are ready to learn *How to Live the Supernatural Life in the Here and Now!*

Dreams and Visions Volume 1

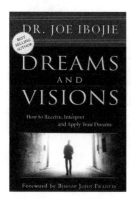

Dreams and Visions presents sound scriptural principles and practical instructions to help you understand dreams and visions. The book provides readers with the necessary understanding to approach dreams and visions by the Holy Spirit, through biblical illustrations, understanding of the meaning of dreams and prophetic symbolism, and by exploring the art of dream interpretation according to ancient methods of the Bible.

BEST SELLERS BY DR. JOE IBOJIE

ILLUSTRATED BIBLE-BASED DICTIONARY OF DREAM SYMBOLS

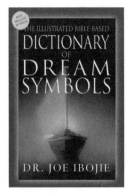

This book is a companion to *Dreams & Visions: How to Receive, Interpret and Apply Your Dreams* and will help today's believers understand what dream symbols mean. When used through the Holy Spirit, it can help the reader take away the frustration of not knowing what dreams mean and avoid the dangers of misinterpretation.

—Joseph Ewen
Founder and Leader of Riverside Church Network
Banff, Scotland, UK

This book is a treasure chest, loaded down with revelation and the hidden mysteries of God that have been waiting since before the foundation of the earth to be uncovered. *Illustrated Bible-Based Dictionary of Dream Symbols* shall bless, strengthen, and guide any believer who is in search for the purpose, promise, and destiny of God for their lives.

—Bishop Ron Scott Jr.
President, Kingdom Coalition International
Hagerstown, Maryland

Illustrated Bible-Based Dictionary of Dream Symbols is much more than a book of dream symbols; it has also added richness to our reading of God's Word. Whether you use this book to assist in interpreting your dreams or as an additional resource for your study of the Word of God, you will find it a welcome companion.

—Robert and Joyce Ricciardelli
Directors, Visionary Advancement Strategies
Seattle, Washington

DREAMS AND VISIONS 2

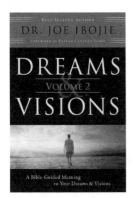

God speaks to you through dreams and visions. Do you want to know the meaning of your dreams? Do you want to know what He is telling and showing you? Now you can know!

Dreams and Visions Volume 2 is packed full of exciting and bible-guided ways to discover the meaning of your God-inspired, dreamy nighttime adventures and your wide-awake supernatural experiences!

Dr. Joe Ibojie reveals why and how God wants to communicate with you through dreams and visions. In this *second volume*, the teaching emphasizes how to gain clearer understanding of your dreams and visions in a new, in-depth, and user-friendly way.

BIBLE-BASED DICTIONARY OF PROPHETIC SYMBOLS FOR EVERY CHRISTIAN

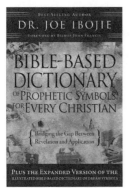

The most comprehensive, illustrated Bible-based dictionary of prophetic and dream symbols ever compiled is contained in this one authoritative book!

The Bible-Based Dictionary of Prophetic Symbols for Every Christian is a masterpiece that intelligently and understandably bridges the gap between prophetic revelation and application—PLUS it includes the expanded version of the best selling *Illustrated Bible-Based Dictionary of Dream Symbols.*

Expertly designed, researched, and Holy Spirit inspired to provide you an extensive wealth of revelation knowledge about symbols and symbolic actions, this book is divided into four parts that go way beyond listing and defining words. Rhema word and divine prompting lift off every page!

NEW AND EXCITING TITLES BY DR. JOE IBOJIE

THE WATCHMAN
THE MINISTRY OF THE SEER IN A LOCAL CHURCH

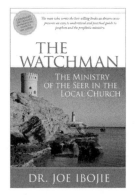

The ministry of the watchman in a local church is possibly one of the most common and yet one of the most misunderstood ministries in the Body of Christ. Over time, the majority of these gifted people have been driven into reclusive lives because of relational issues and confusion surrounding their very vital ministry in the local church.

Through the pages of *The Watchman* you will learn:

- Who these watchmen are.
- How they can be recognized, trained, appreciated, and integrated into the Body of Christ.
- About their potential and how they can be channelled as valuable resources to the local leadership.
- How to avoid prophetic and pastoral pitfalls.
- How to receive these gifted folks as the oracles of God they really are.

The 21st century watchman ministry needs a broader and clearer definition. It is time that the conservative, narrow, and restrictive perspectives of the watchman's ministry be enlarged into the reality of its great potential and value God has intended.

THE FINAL FRONTIERS
COUNTDOWN TO THE FINAL SHOWDOWN

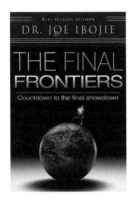

The maladies that define the focal feature of our existence are that we face a continuous threat from the challenges of the earth in a fallen state. Every now and again, we witness the eruptions of nature against man with catastrophic consequences, but these are only miniature representations of an immense cosmic cataclysm that could occur. Gradually the things that make the earth precious to us are disappearing with few taking notice. *The Final Frontiers* is a peep into the future and a call to action. It provides you with a practical approach to the changing struggles that confront humanity now and in your future and reveals through Scriptures and modern-day experiences:

- What was lost at the Fall
- The elements of nature in God's service
- How to defeat the devil at the mind game
- Invisible realms of hell
- Spiritual weaponry
- Peace and the ultimate redemption

"In writing this book, I feel like the prophet Jeremiah, calling humanity to be alert to the ploy of the enemy, to break the secret bubble, and reveal the shapes of warfare to come." —Dr. Joe Ibojie

DREAM COURSES

DREAMS ARE THE PARABLE LANGUAGE of God in a world that is spiritually distancing itself from experiencing the reality of His Presence. They are personalized, coded messages from God. Through dreams, God breaks through our thought processes, mindsets, prejudices and emotions to connect with the spirit of man. In this way He shows us what we might have missed or not heard or what our natural mind was incapable of comprehending. We all dream. He speaks to us at our individual levels and leads us further in Christ. God's ultimate purpose in dreams and visions is to align us to His plan and purposes in our lives!

The purpose of these courses is to equip the saints for the end-time move of God by learning the art of hearing Him and understanding how He speaks through dreams at an individual level.

Each dream course builds on the knowledge gained in the previous course. Attendees are strongly encouraged to take the courses in order for maximum effectiveness.

Topics covered include:

COURSE 1

- Introduction to dreams and visions.
- Biblical history of dreams and visions.
- How dreams are received.

- Hindrances to receiving and remembering your dreams.
- How to respond to your dreams.
- Differences between dreams and visions.
- Introduction to interpreting your dreams.
- Understanding the ministry of angels.

Course 2

- Introduction to the language of symbols (the language of the spirit).
- Different levels of interpretation of dreams.
- Why we seek the meaning of our dreams.
- What to do with dreams you do not immediately understand.
- Maintaining and developing your dream-life.
- Expanding the scope of your dreams.
- Improving your interpretative skill.
- Visions and the Third Heaven.

Course 3

- Responding to revelations.
- Interpreting the dreams of others.
- Guidelines for setting up a corporate dream group.
- Prophetic symbolism.
- How to organize Dream Workshops.
- The Seer's anointing.
- The ministry of a Watchman.
- Spiritual warfare (fighting the good fight).
- Understanding the roles of angels and the different categories of angelic forces.
- How to work with angels.

COURSE 4

- Living the supernatural in the natural.
- Understanding the spiritual senses.
- Maintaining balance while blending the natural and the spiritual senses.
- Security and information management in revelatory ministry.
- Understanding the anointing.
- Dialoguing with God.
- An anatomy of scriptural dreams.

WEEKEND COURSES

Friday

- Registration begins at 5:00 P.M.
- Teaching begins at 6:00 P.M.

Saturday

- Registration begins at 9:00 A.M.
- Sessions begin at 10:30 A.M., 1:30 P.M. and 7:00 P.M.

One Week Course (Monday through Friday)

Courses begin Monday morning and conclude Friday evening.
- Registration begins each day at 9:00 A.M.
- Sessions begin at 10:00 A.M. and end at 5:00 P.M.

There are breaks for lunch and tea.

The contents of each Dream Course will be covered in two weekend courses or a single one-week course (Monday through Friday).

To Request a DREAM COURSE in your area of the world, PLEASE CALL TO ARRANGE A PROGRAM TO FIT YOUR NEEDS:

Dr. Joe Ibojie
info@the-fathers-house.org.uk
44-1224-701343
44-7765-834253